KITCHEN WORKSHOP

PIZZA

Hands-on Cooking Lessons for Making Amazing Pizza at Home

RUTH GRESSER

Quarry Books
100 Cummings Center, Suite 406L
Beverly, MA 01915

quarrybooks.com • quarryspoon.com

First published in the United States of America in 2014 by
Quarry Books, a member of
Quayside Publishing Group
100 Cummings Center
Suite 406-L
Beverly, Massachusetts 01915-6101
Telephone: (978) 282-9590
Fax: (978) 283-2742
www.quarrybooks.com
Visit www.QuarrySPOON.com and help us celebrate food and culture one spoonful at a time!

10 9 8 7 6 5 4 3 2 1

ISBN: 978-1-59253-883-6

Digital edition published in 2014
eISBN: 978-1-61058-897-3

Library of Congress Cataloging-in-Publication Data
Gresser, Ruth.
  Kitchen workshop--pizza : hands-on cooking lessons for making amazing pizza at home / Ruth
Gresser.
    pages cm
  ISBN 978-1-59253-883-6 (pbk.)
1. Pizza. I. Title. II. Title: Pizza.
  TX770.P58.G74 2014
  641.82'48--dc23
                                                                            2013038896

Cover and Book Design: Debbie Berne
Cover Image: Moshe Zusman
Page Layout: Sporto
Concept and Recipe Development Collaboration: Bonnie Moore
Paintings on pages 3 and 158: Barbara Johnson
Graphic on page 8: Leanne Poteet
Beer Cooler Collaboration: Greg Jasgur

Printed in China

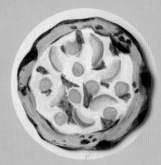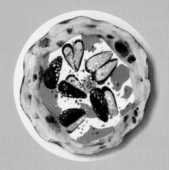

To Marty, my partner in
food, art, and joy.

CONTENTS

INTRODUCTION

Everybody loves pizza. Your love of pizza brings you to this book because you want to conquer the challenge of making pizzeria-quality pizza at home. My love of pizza took me to a career of pizza making. For over 20 years, I have owned and operated one of the nation's top pizza restaurants, Pizzeria Paradiso, with several locations in the Washington, D.C., metropolitan area. Relying on my many years of pizza-making experience, I created this book to help guide you on your quest to make great-tasting pizza.

Pizzeria Paradiso's pizza begins with Neapolitan ideas and crosses the ocean to include American techniques and ingredients. But Pizzeria Paradiso–style pizza isn't the only pizza in town. That's why in this book I will teach you to make not only standard pizzas from the Pizzeria Paradiso menu but also a variety of pizzas, from Neapolitan to New York, from classic to modern, and from simple to complex.

In eighteenth-century Naples, tomatoes—recently imported from the New World—lost their poisonous reputation and the first tomato-topped pies appeared. Soon after, the addition of cheese completed today's most accepted definition of pizza. As modern pizza circled the globe, its transformation continued. The basic ingredients remained the same, but it took on local touches. In America, for example, pizzas got bigger and more heavily topped. This book's opening chapters offer variations on the classic definition of pizza. The later chapters enter the realm of the unexpected with sauces and toppings that demonstrate pizza's transformation, stimulate your imagination, and motivate you to experiment.

Though pizza is a simple food, it may require a little effort to develop the level of competency necessary to produce the results you desire. I listened as my recipe testers relayed their challenges and successes. I was gratified to hear that with time they all felt accomplished in their pizza-making goal. As my mother said, "Doing [it] develops technique and comfort" with the process and the product. Several people tested recipes by having a party with friends and family, thus revealing pizza's communal character and yet another level of pizza's appeal.

At Pizzeria Paradiso, we developed an extensive program that explores another aspect of pizza's appeal: its affinity for beer. Through a constantly changing draft beer menu as well as upward of 200 bottled beers, we offer a vast selection of the world's greatest and most unique beers. Greg Jasgur, Pizzeria Paradiso's executive bar manager, worked with me to fashion beer pairings for a number of the pizzas in this book. Called "Greg's Beer Cooler," each pairing includes a style of beer appropriate for a given pizza as well as "Greg's Pick"—his favorite beer to drink with that pie.

No matter how you like it, what you drink with it, or how pizza changes over time, the fundamental truth of pizza remains: It is the people's food. As a meal in itself that can easily contain all five food groups (grain, vegetables, fruits, proteins, and dairy), pizza ranks at the top of most people's list of favorite foods. And the best part is, you can eat it with your fingers.

At Pizzeria Paradiso, our "Eat your pizza" slogan has welcomed guests since the day we fired up the pizza oven and opened our doors. Now, you can not only "Eat your pizza," but you can "Make your pizza" as well. I hope you have fun with the process and enjoy every bite.

—Ruth Gresser

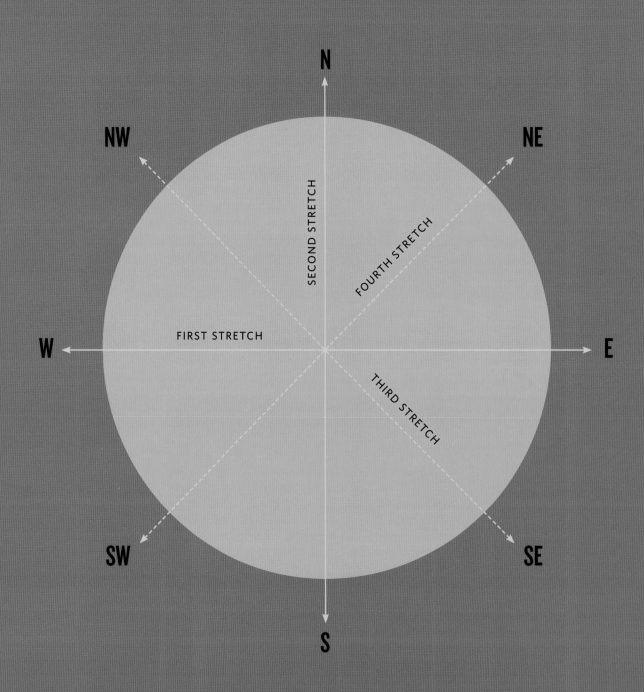

THE WHAT AND HOW OF MAKING PIZZA

Don't start making pizza before you read this chapter!

A good pizza depends on ingredients, equipment, methods, and taste. In the following pages, you will find basic information to help you make choices regarding equipment and ingredients. You will also find detailed instructions on methods that you can apply to the recipes throughout the book. By adding the fundamentals you learn in this chapter to your own personal tastes, you will have a solid foundation upon which to create the delicious pizzas you desire.

Joy infused the progress reports of the 20-plus pizza testers who worked their way through the techniques and recipes of this book. We shared a mutual giddiness with each step forward, with every positive result, and with each skill mastered. Many had never made dough, or pizza, at home before. In the words of one tester, "It was like taking a course in gourmet pizza making." As you make your way through this chapter and the pizzas that follow, I trust the giddiness that I shared with my recipe testers will bubble up in you as well.

THE EQUIPMENT YOU'LL NEED

Having the right equipment will not only make pizza making easier, but it will also make your pizza better. Besides the standard cooking equipment found in most kitchens, the shortlist of essential equipment for pizza making follows:

- **Kitchen scale:** This is used to measure the flour for the dough as well as various toppings. This scale should measure to the 1/4 ounce (7 g).

- **Dough scraper:** This metal or plastic tool allows you to manipulate your ingredients as you make your dough.

- **Pizza peel:** This is a wood slab with a handle for building your pies. Make sure its width is big enough for the size of the pie you want to make. The recipes in this book make 12-inch (30 cm) pizzas.

- **Pizza stone:** Place this square or round stone tile in the oven during preheating. It will help crisp the bottom of your pizzas while they bake. You can purchase a stone designed specifically for pizza baking, or you can purchase a low-fire ceramic or brick tile from a hardware store. You can also try using a pizza steel or baking steel—a relatively new pizza-baking tile made of metal—in place of the pizza stone.

- **Oven:** Wood, gas, and electric ovens all work as long as the temperature is constant and reaches 500° to 900°F (260°C to 482°C, or gas mark 10 or higher).

If you make your pizza dough by hand, top it with crushed fresh tomatoes, olive oil, salt, and pepper and then bake. That's all you'll need. It's pure, simple perfection without embellishment!

Most of the dough recipes call for an electric mixer, but you can make the doughs by hand if you choose. If you use an electric mixer, you will want one that mixes at both very slow and faster speeds and comes with a dough hook. The Deep Dish (page 49) requires a 10-inch (25.5 cm) round baking pan or skillet 1 1/2 to 2 inches (3.8 to 5 cm) deep. I like to use my cast-iron skillet for the perfect deep-dish pie.

METHODS TO MASTER

This is pizza making, not brain surgery, a Supreme Court argument, or rocket science. Nonetheless, pizza making, like these other endeavors, has a skill set that needs mastery. Here are some details to help you develop your skills.

How to Plan Your Pizza-Making Adventure

Some of the recipes in this book take just a couple of hours to prepare. Others take longer, and a couple (only a couple) take 2 to 3 days. Even though most of that time is devoted to the dough's rising, I cannot stress enough the importance of doing a little planning before you enter the kitchen. I don't want you to discover at 6 o'clock that your pizza won't be ready for your guests' arrival at 8. So, always read through the entire recipe before you start and plan your preparation so that it works for your schedule.

Consider organizing your pizza preparations over several days. You can start the dough-making process for most of the doughs 2 to 3 days before you want to make pizza. For the more involved pizzas, one possible and painless way to plan your pizza-making fun is to make the dough on day one, prepare your toppings on day two, and make your pizza on day three. I don't want to scare you, though. Many of these pizzas can easily be made in an afternoon.

How to Make and Work with Pizza Dough

As you progress through the recipes in this book, you will most likely find that making the crust is the most challenging endeavor. The process is relatively simple even though it includes a number of steps over an extended period. The dough recipes detail the process for each type of crust. Here I want to cover information common to all.

Let's start with a few easy tips. When working with dough, you'll find that having one clean hand makes the process easier. So, when possible, make one hand your work hand and one hand your clean, or at least cleaner, hand. Then you will have a clean hand free to answer the phone—or so said Julia Child, as the story goes.

Also, if you find yourself with doughy hands that need cleaning, don't simply go to the sink and wash your hands. First take a healthy bit of flour and rub your hands together over your trash bin. This will remove most of the dough bits from your hands. Follow this with a soap-and-water wash at the sink. Similarly, when cleaning your counter after making dough, first scrape the counter with a dough scraper to remove most of the dough stuck to the counter. Scrape this residue into the trash, not into your sink. Next,

wipe the counter with cold water and then wipe again with warm soap and water. These two simple tips will save your sink drain from clogging with pizza dough.

Always take a good deal of care when measuring the ingredients for making your dough. Each recipe has dough mixing, kneading, and rising times designed for and essential to the character of each crust. Each recipe also includes a room temperature rising time and a refrigerated rising time. Using the longer, slower, cooler process of letting the dough rise in the refrigerator will allow the dough to develop a yeastier flavor in your crust.

How to Proof Yeast

Dissolve the yeast in warm water (about 105°F or 41°C) and let it stand for 5 to 10 minutes. This process is done to ensure that the yeast is viable and will leaven your pizza dough. You will notice small bubbles from, or a slight creaminess in, the yeast after it dissolves in the warm water. This shows that the yeast is alive and will do the job you need it to do. Some newer recipes skip this step, but I think giving the yeast a little time to develop before incorporating it into the flour makes for a more consistent and reliable leaven.

How to Shape the Dough for the Second Rise

You will shape the dough into balls for the second rise, by moving your hands in a gentle, yet confident, cupping, curving motion.

1) On a lightly-floured counter, place your hands on either side of the piece of dough, cradling it slightly at the bottom where it meets the work surface .

2) Exerting a little inward and downward pressure on both sides, begin to turn the dough counterclockwise **(A)**. Continue turning and pushing inward and downward toward the center of the dough.

3) The dough should stick slightly to the work surface at the center of the bottom of the ball. The spot where the dough sticks to the work surface becomes the center point of the ball that will form in 5 or 6 fluid movements **(B)**.

A B

How to Stretch the Dough

Master this section and you master the method of creating round pizza. Before you begin, I have one thought for you to remember as you stretch your first, or your seven hundredth, pizza round: Pizza dough is extremely forgiving. Do not let it scare you. Handle it with confidence and assertiveness. You will not hurt it. If you stretch it and it tears, simply patch it by taking one edge of the hole, pulling it across (closing the hole), and pressing it onto the other side of the hole **(A)**.

If, as you work the dough, you notice it getting less cooperative and harder to manipulate, walk away. Take a piece of plastic wrap or a damp towel and lay it on the dough. Then, let it rest for 10 minutes to let the gluten relax. It will handle better after you both have taken a break. You will notice a great improvement in your skill level around the fourth or fifth time you work with the dough. To stretch the dough, follow these instructions:

1) Using your fingertips, flatten each ball all over until it is 8 inches (20 cm) in diameter **(B)**. Press the dough evenly while maintaining the circular shape.

2) Lift the dough off the counter and slip your fingers under it on opposite sides of the round. Think of your hands as points on a compass (see page 8). Hold the dough between your fingers and thumb on the east and west points and stretch slightly **(C)**. Lay the dough down on the counter and turn the dough a quarter turn. Lift the dough, hold it between your fingers and thumb on the new east and west points, and stretch slightly **(D)**. You've now stretched north, south, east, and west. Lay the dough down on the counter. Turn it an eighth of a turn. Lift the dough and stretch

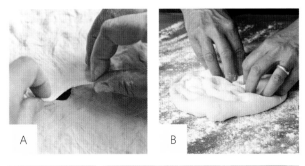

A

B

C

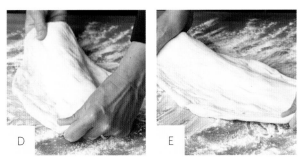

D

E

F

again. Once again, lay the dough down on the counter and make another quarter turn. Then lift the dough and make one final stretch (**E**). With this last stretch, you will have completed stretching the dough round at each of the eight principal points on a compass. Lay the dough back down on the floured surface. The dough round will now measure about 10 inches (25.5 cm) in diameter.

3) Using the fingertips of your first two fingers and your thumbs and placing them about ³/₄ inch (about 2 cm) from the edge of the dough, lift a section of the dough from the surface of the countertop (**F**). Gently stretch the dough by pulling your hands apart. Continue stretching the outer edge of the dough, section by section, letting the dough hang until you have made your way around the full circumference. By letting the dough hang, you use the weight of the dough to help the stretching process. Watch your finger placement as you make your way around the dough. You want the outer edge to remain thicker than the center so that it can form a nice *corona* (Italian for "crown") of crust for the finished pizza. The dough should now be a well-formed round shape measuring 12 inches (30 cm) in diameter. If your dough is slightly misshapen, simply reshape it by pushing (or pulling) the edge until you achieve the desired round pizza shape.

How to Transfer Your Dough to a Pizza Peel

Once you have created your pizza round, you need to move it to the pizza peel to add the toppings. Before you do that, though, you must prepare the peel by scattering cornmeal on it (**A**). The cornmeal will help prevent the dough from sticking to the peel. If you prefer, you can use flour in place of the cornmeal, but cornmeal provides a more substantial layer between the peel and the dough, making things easier for first-time pizza makers.

If your dough sits on the counter for an extended length of time (the phone rings or the dog needs to go out) before you transfer it, sprinkle a little more flour on the underside of your dough before placing it on the peel. Similarly, if as you transfer the dough to the peel you find that the dough is sticky and does not release easily from your fingers, sprinkle more flour on the underside of the dough. You can do this by picking up one part of the dough at a time and sprinkling flour onto the counter (or more flour or cornmeal on the peel) and then laying the dough back down on top of the flour.

To transfer the pizza round to the peel, follow these instructions:

1) Using the fingertips of your left hand, lift the edge of the dough that is furthest away from you. Then, slide your right hand, with your palm up, underneath the dough to the east point on the compass, keeping your thumb on the top of the round of dough. Next, lift the thumb of your left hand off the top of the dough. Slide your left hand, again palm up, under the dough to the west point on the compass so that the fingertips of both hands point toward each other.

2) Keeping your hands flat and parallel to the countertop, lift your hands straight up until they are a few inches off the counter. The dough will come off the counter and hang down off the edge of your hands (**B**).

A

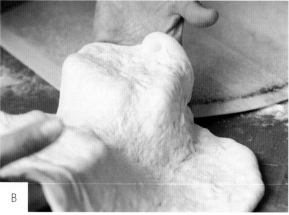

B

3) Move your hands (and the dough) over to your prepared peel (**C**) and lower your hands until they are just above the center of the peel (**D**).

4) Slide your hands out from the underside of the dough. The dough round will drop onto the peel. If necessary, reshape the dough into a round.

C

D

How to Top Your Pizza

Once you have your pizza dough on your pizza peel, you want to get your pizza into the oven as quickly as possible. So, plan ahead, making sure you have your toppings ready before you stretch your dough—all of your toppings, from sauce to salt to oil. Then top your pizza gently, confidently, and quickly. The longer your pizza sits on the peel, the more trouble you will have getting it into the oven. Three key points: Don't press down when spreading the sauce, don't press the toppings into the dough, and put the pizza in the oven as soon as you finish adding the toppings.

The recipes in this book vary widely in the amount of toppings for each pizza. The Pizza Marinara (page 56) gets a simple garnish of toppings, while the Apples pizza (page 144) gets a robust amount of big-flavored fall ingredients. In general, keep the amount of toppings (cheese and sauce included) for a 12-inch (30 cm) pizza to around, or less than, 3 cups (with the exception of raw leafy greens). This guideline ensures that your pizza does not get overburdened.

How to Top Deep-Dish and Gluten-Free Pizzas

Most of the recipes in this book make one 12-inch (30 cm) pizza. The Deep Dish recipe, however, makes a 10-inch (25.5 cm) pizza, and the Gluten-Free recipe makes a 9-inch (23 cm) pizza. Should you want to adapt one of the 12-inch (30 cm) pizza recipes to make a deep-dish pizza, you will want to double the amount of cheese and sauce and use only half to two-thirds of the other toppings. The most appropriate recipes for this conversion are those with big flavors that can shine on a robust crust. For gluten-free pizza, you will want to decrease all toppings by about one-third. Recipes most suited for adapting to a gluten-free crust will have sauce of one sort or another and moist toppings.

How to Put the Pizza into the Oven

In every recipe except the Deep Dish, just before each pizza slides off the peel onto your pizza stone, the instructions tell you to "give the peel a quick shake." Do not skip or forget this step in your zeal to put the pizza in the oven. Even a quickly, lightly, and gently topped pizza can stick to the peel, resulting in a pizza that doesn't slip gracefully into the oven.

A few pointers will help a novice pizza maker master this movement. First, practice the shake with an empty peel. Lay the peel on your counter. Grasp the handle of the peel and, in a quick, confident movement of your wrist, push the peel away about 6 inches (15 cm) and bring it back toward you to its original spot.

Once you feel you've mastered the movement, make your pizza. With the pizza now in place on the peel, repeat the motion (A). You want to see the pizza move slightly and with ease. If it does, move on to the oven.

If, even with all your planning, your pizza does not move on the peel when you shake the peel, lift a piece of the edge of the dough off of the peel and scatter a little more cornmeal onto the peel (B). Lay the dough back down and redistribute the toppings. Give a shake again. If necessary, add more cornmeal under another section of the pizza. With a bit of coaxing, and a good deal of patience, you'll get any pizza moving about on the peel so that one swift shake will cause it to glide easily onto your stone.

Once you have the pizza freely moving about the peel, open the oven door and pull the rack out slightly. Place the tip of the peel at the far end of the pizza stone so that the peel rests at a 20-degree angle to the stone and so the pizza itself (still on the peel) sits directly above the stone (C). With one swift motion, pull the peel out from under the pizza. The pizza will drop directly onto the stone. Quickly push in the rack and close the oven door (or leave it slightly ajar on electric ovens).

A

B

C

How to Bake Your Pizza

The best pizza cooks at a high temperature. Pizzerias use special pizza ovens, whether coal-, gas-, or wood-fired, that reach 650°F (343°C) or more. To make pizza at home, I have developed a technique that will replicate pizzeria-style pizza in a home oven.

When you read the recipes, you will note that I have you bake the pizza on a pizza stone and set the oven to broil to preheat the pizza stone. You will also begin cooking the pizza with the oven still set to broil. This is very important because the pizza needs to start cooking at an intense heat level that most home ovens can produce most efficiently on the broil setting.

Mastering this high-temperature method of baking depends on knowing your oven and the best way to get to, and maintain, the highest temperature possible. Many ovens today have automatic shut-off features that turn the oven off after a specific amount of time or once the oven reaches a pre-set temperature. For instance, my broiler shuts off after about 45 minutes. So, I've learned that I need to preheat my oven and broil my pizza within that 45-minute window.

Other ovens have broilers that cycle on and off when they reach certain temperatures. If your broiler cycles off at a lower temperature than the highest bake setting for your oven, then regardless of my instruction, preheat your oven and pizza stone on the highest bake setting rather than on the broiler setting.

No matter how you preheat your oven and stone, you will begin the baking process under the heat of the broiler. If you preheat your oven and stone at the highest bake setting, switch your oven to broil before sliding the pizza into the oven. Also, check that the broiler element turns on before you put in your pizza. In the first minute or two of baking, the pizza gets the intense burst of heat possible only through direct exposure to the heat of the broiler.

When you want to bake more than one pizza in succession, always allow the oven and pizza stone to come back up to temperature before making the next pie. Also, after removing one pizza from the oven, you will want to scrape off and discard any cornmeal that remains on the stone. If you leave the cornmeal, it might burn before, or during, the next pizza's baking, which could give the pizza a bitter taste.

How to Use Your Pizza Stone

The first step in most of the pizza recipes in this book instructs you to "place a pizza stone on the top rack of a cool oven." Please take care to ensure that your oven is *cool*. Also, after washing your stone, let it dry completely before using it. Your stone must be completely *dry* before you use it. Not paying attention to these two conditions could cause your stone to crack, making its pizza-baking days a thing of the past.

Some recipes require baking or roasting a topping in the oven prior to baking the pizza. Since the stone needs to go into a cold oven, the recipe will always instruct you to place the stone in the oven before you preheat the oven to cook the toppings. The stone is not relevant to the cooking of the toppings. This process simply ensures that the stone preheats in a cold oven.

Finally, the recipes instruct you to place the pizza stone on the top rack of your oven. The stone should generally sit about 4 inches (10 cm) from the heat source. If the top rack of your oven sits less than 4 inches (10 cm) from the broiler, place the stone on a rack seated on the second glide from the top. Of course, some ovens have broilers with less intense heat sources. If your oven does not begin to brown the pizza and the *corona* (the outer ring of crust) does not puff while the pizza bakes on the broiler setting, on your next attempt, move your stone closer to the broiler element.

How to Bake Pizza in an Electric Oven

For those of you with electric ovens, keep your oven door slightly ajar (about 2 inches, or 5 cm) when you have the oven set to broil—both during the preheating (if preheating on broil) and during the initial pizza baking. With the oven door open, the broiler element stays on and continues heating. If you close the oven door, the oven will hit a pre-set temperature limit that turns off the broiler element, thus shutting down the source of heat. Remember to close the oven door completely when you turn the oven to the highest bake setting (and if you preheat on the bake setting) or else too much heat will escape.

How to Bake Your Pizza in an Oven with a Drawer Broiler

If your oven has a drawer broiler, place the pizza stone on the top shelf of your oven and preheat your oven and the pizza stone on the broil setting for 1 hour. There is a good chance that your oven will reach a temperature of 550°F (288°C) or more. You can check the temperature with an oven thermometer. If the oven temperature reaches this level of heat, bake the pizza on the top rack of your oven, with the oven set to broil for the complete baking process.

If, on the other hand, your oven does not reach 550°F (288°C) or more, then move the stone to the broiler drawer. Set the stone on the broiler pan, 4 inches (10 cm) from the flame, and follow the broil instructions. After the initial broil step, move the broiler pan with the pizza stone on it to the top rack of the oven chamber. Turn your oven setting to its highest bake setting and continue cooking as instructed in the recipe. Please be sure to use heavy oven mitts for this step, as the pizza stone and broiler pan will be extremely hot.

How to Bake Your Pizza in an Oven with No Broiler

These ovens represent the biggest challenge to baking pizzeria-style pizza. If your oven does not have a broiler, preheat the oven on its highest bake setting for up to 1 hour (making sure that your oven does not have an automatic time or temperature shut off) and then bake the pizza. You will most likely need to bake your pizza for 15 to 20 minutes rather than the 10 minutes in the instructions.

A

B

How to Turn Your Pizza

In every recipe except the Deep Dish, halfway through the cooking of the pizza, the instructions read "rotate the pizza, not the stone, a half turn." You turn the pizza to ensure that, particularly at this high temperature, the pizza cooks evenly and doesn't burn on one side. This step will become second nature to you. You may even get to the point where you no longer reach for the tongs to perform this step and use your fingers instead. Nonetheless, in the beginning, this may give you pause. Fear not: By this stage in the cooking process, the pizza will have become firm and easy to manipulate. With a pair of tongs, grasp the edge of the pizza at the East point (on your pizza compass) and turn that spot to the South point **(A)**. Repeat the same movement a second time.

How to Know When Your Pizza Is Done

You will see from the images in this book that I like some char to my pizzas. You may or may not like this flavor quality, and you should make your pizza according to your tastes. Ideally, if your pizza stone received a lengthy preheating and your oven maintained its high temperature, your pizzas will emerge with a crisp and gently browned bottom crust, a slightly charred upper crust, and thoroughly cooked, melted, and slightly browned toppings. If at the end of the prescribed length of cooking the pizza has not reached this stage, leave it in the oven for another couple of minutes. When the pizza reaches this level of doneness, remove it from the oven and enjoy!

How to Remove Your Pizza from the Oven

Use a pair of tongs and your peel to remove your pizza from the oven. Using the tongs, pick up the closest edge of the pizza and simply slide your peel under it. Push the peel until it slides fully under the entire pizza **(B)**. Next, lift the peel from the stone and remove it, and the pizza it carries, from the oven.

INGREDIENTS TO CHOOSE

Here are some of the considerations you'll want to make when selecting your ingredients.

Dough Ingredients

The most traditional pizza dough combines just four ingredients. The ingredient list varies and swells as you veer away from tradition and in turn influences method, texture, and flavor.

Flour
Wheat flour is the major ingredient in pizza dough; that's simple enough. From there nothing is simple. Flour decisions range from the protein content (the softer, or lower protein, flours include European type "00" flour and American all-purpose flour, while durum flour is the highest in protein, or hardest) to organic to whole grain. Another option, sprouted flour, proves easier to digest and therefore offers beneficial nutritional results. While you will find a measure of uniformity in flour, it does vary according to its source and its grind. Try various flours until you find the one that performs best for you.

Most of the recipes indicate a particular choice of flour. If availability problems exist, all-purpose flour, true to its name, can be substituted. The results may vary from what the recipe as written would produce, but you can still make delicious pizza.

You will notice that I instruct you to weigh the flour rather than measuring the flour by volume. I do this to ensure a level of consistency in the amount of flour used. Volume measurement does not afford the same accuracy due to the variation in flour grinds, the settling of the grains of flour in the storage package or container, and the way you spoon it out.

Yeast
The single-cell organisms that create alcohol and bread and make your pizza rise come in several different forms. Most of the recipes in this book use active dry yeast. Substitutions include fast-rising active dry yeast, compressed fresh yeast, or fresh or soured sponges and starters. The most important thing about yeast is its vitality. Your job is to feed and nourish it to keep it alive so it can do the job of leavening the dough.

Water
Much is said about water, including claims that to make true New York pizza you must use New York water. I will not confirm or refute that point. Nonetheless, I will say that the two most important things for me about the water in pizza dough are the amount and the temperature. I prefer a moist, supple dough, which requires the addition of more water than may be expected. The temperature relates to the yeast—remember, warm but not hot water, or you will kill your sacred friend the yeast organism and your dough will not rise.

Oil
To fat or not to fat: this is the next question. The answer depends again on the dough you wish to create. True Neapolitan pizza contains no fat, while Chicago deep-dish pizza contains a surprising amount. I generally suggest extra-virgin olive oil if and when you choose to use fat.

Salt
There are a plethora of salts available today, from ordinary iodized table salt to kosher salt to unrefined mineral-rich varietal salts. Choose according to your tastes and pocketbook, but remember that the healthier salts are the unrefined ones. I specify kosher salt in most recipes. If you use a different type of salt, you may need to use more or less depending on the grind and the type.

Other

Purists will stop reading here, saying that pizza dough should contain nothing else. But you can expand your dough larder if you choose. Many pizza doughs contain sugar or other sweeteners, while health-conscious cooks add or substitute grains (whole and refined) other than wheat. Herbs, spices, citrus peel, fruit juices, garlic, and onions can also add flavor to pizza dough if you want to venture away from the traditional.

Sauce and Toppings

Below, you'll find general information about some of the toppings that appear on the pizzas throughout this book.

Tomatoes

You will find a surprising number of options when choosing the type of tomato to top your pizza. You can lay freshly sliced tomatoes on your pizza as it comes out of the oven at the height of summer, or you can choose a simple canned San Marzano sauce in the dead of winter. In this book, I use several kinds of canned tomatoes and fresh tomatoes.

The overarching rule for fresh tomatoes is to use them at the height of their season and to handle them gently. Canned tomatoes vary greatly from producer to producer, so try a selection and let your taste buds make the choice.

Canned tomatoes also come processed in different ways. In general, I call for canned whole tomatoes and instruct you to crush them by hand. Occasionally, I call for canned crushed tomatoes. The two products differ greatly, with the canned crushed tomatoes having a saucier consistency. You may substitute one for the other, but you will need more whole tomatoes to replace a given amount of crushed tomatoes. Last, I use sun-dried tomatoes to impart a deep, rich tomato essence.

Tomato Sauce

The first chapter of this book contains seven different tomato sauces, each bringing an individual flair to the pizzas they adorn. The sauces range from the simple to the complex, from little to no cooking to multiple levels of cooking. Try one, or all, and choose a favorite, or use one of your own.

Cheese

As a mainstay topping for pizza, cheese might seem like a throwaway item, not deserving of attention. I hope to change your perspective if you hold this view. I use nearly 20 different cheeses in this book, chosen specifically to complement the other ingredients on the pizza. Since it is such a significant topping, I always advise that you use the best quality cheese available. Feel free to mix and match cheeses based on your taste preferences.

Mozzarella Cheese

You will find both fresh cow milk mozzarella and buffalo milk mozzarella (cheese generally imported from Italy made from the milk of domesticated water buffalo) called for in this book. Cow milk mozzarella, easier to locate than buffalo mozzarella, is less creamy and milder in flavor than the buffalo variety. You can substitute one for the other in most of the recipes. When you use cow's milk mozzarella, try to locate the more flavorful and fatty fresh cheese rather than aged mozzarella. *Fresh* mozzarella often comes packed in a brine. If you use this type, always drain and pat it dry before using.

Pecorino Cheese

Pecorino cheese is simply a cheese made from sheep's milk. I specify the use of Pecorino Toscano, a nutty, firm but not hard cheese that melts well. Do not substitute Pecorino Romano, as it will be too strong, too salty, and it will not melt properly. However, you may substitute any nutty melting cheese, such as Petit Basque, for the Pecorino Toscano.

Olive Oil

Most of the pizzas in this book get a drizzle of olive oil before heading into the oven. At Pizzeria Paradiso, we also drizzle oil on most of our pizzas when they emerge from the oven. We use extra-virgin olive oil with a flavor that we enjoy for this step, as it is considered the highest quality olive oil available. You may choose to use only extra-virgin olive oil as well. Keep in mind that with the enormous number and variety of olive oils available, just choosing an extra-virgin olive oil may not be enough to ensure that you like the flavor. Since you add the oil primarily to enhance the flavor of the pizza, it is most important that you like the flavor of the oil you are using. So, taste different olive oils until you find an oil that you enjoy.

Onions

At Pizzeria Paradiso, we use red onions to top our pizzas. Red onions provide a milder onion flavor than standard yellow onions, while not falling into the sweet onion category. Red onions, with their purple hue, also offer a visual spark to many of the pizzas. You can follow our lead or make an onion choice of your own.

Sausage

Both pork and lamb sausage appear in the recipes in this book. You can substitute other types of your choosing. You can also use stuffed link sausages in place of the loose bulk sausage as specified in the recipes, using them sliced raw or precooked to top your pie. Whichever you use, keep the pieces of raw sausage that dot the pizza small (no more than 1/3 inch, or 1 cm) to ensure that they cook fully during the relatively short pizza cooking time. I also have you add the sausage last when topping the pizza to ensure that the sausage cooks completely in the oven. If you are concerned about the sausage fully cooking or if you prefer to reduce the amount of fat that the sausage imparts to the pizza, you can instead choose to cook the sausage partially or completely before using it to top the pie.

Prosciutto

When possible, choose imported Italian prosciutto di Parma. This special ham is dry cured and lightly salted and has a wonderfully robust, musky flavor.

Anchovies

Preserved anchovies offer a depth of flavor to some of the sauces and pizzas in this book. Many people shy away from anchovies. I encourage you not to do so and instead suggest that you investigate high-quality anchovies preserved in olive oil or salt. They are generally firmer in texture and subtler and cleaner in flavor than other types, and I think they can make an anchovy appreciator, if not an anchovy lover, out of anyone.

Olives

I call for several types of olives in this book and chose each for its particular flavor. If you have difficulty finding the olive specified, you may substitute another of your choice. When buying olives, I choose olives that have not been pitted because I enjoy their flavor more. I then remove the pits myself. To remove the pits from olives, place the olive on a cutting board and then place the flat side of your knife onto the olive. Hold the knife by the handle with one hand to stabilize the knife. Push down on the flat side of the knife blade with your other hand. You will thus smash the olive between the knife's blade and the cutting board. Using your fingers, you can then squeeze the pit from the olive flesh.

Capers

The flower bud of the caper plant has flavored Italian and Mediterranean foods for centuries. Available pickled in vinegar, packed in oil, or preserved in salt, they add a distinctive, flowery flavor. If you use salted capers, you will need to rinse them and soak them to remove the salt. Rinse the capers, cover with water, soak for 30 minutes, and drain. Repeat twice. The capers are now ready to use. For less residual salt, soak a fourth time.

Herbs

I call for fresh herbs throughout the book. If you substitute dried herbs, the general rule of thumb is to replace the fresh herbs with one third the amount of dried herbs.

Fruits and Vegetables

In this book, I introduce fruits and vegetables that you may never have thought of as pizza toppings. Generally, use fresh, in-season produce and remember to wash all fruits and vegetables before using them.

In a couple of recipes, I call for lemon and orange supremes. To make supremes, cut the top and bottom rinds from the fruit, revealing its flesh. Then, working from the top to bottom and making your way around the circumference of the fruit, cut off the remaining rind (A). Cut the wedges of flesh from between the membranes of each lemon or orange section (B).

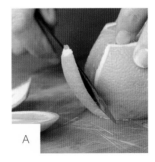
A

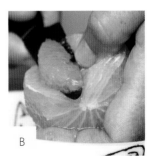
B

PIZZA BASICS

The most universal and basic definition of pizza includes only three elements: dough, tomato, and cheese. While this simple and quintessentially peasant meal defines pizza, variations are limited only by your imagination.

To spark your imagination, you will find in the pages that follow recipes for seven tomato-and-cheese pizzas, each with a different flavor profile. The recipes run the gamut from a classic Neapolitan pizza to the Deep Dish—a true "pie" of a pizza. You can stick to the combinations I suggest or mix and match dough, sauces, and cheeses to develop your own.

As you progress through the recipes, you will become more accomplished and more comfortable with each step of the process. With the skills you develop and the flavor preferences you discover, you can move on from the Basics to the Classics, then through the Pizzeria Paradiso pizzas, and enter a world of your own creations.

THE PARADISO

This dough and sauce have joined to create the pizzas at Pizzeria Paradiso for more than twenty years. I hope you find this pizza as irresistible as our customers do.

Paradiso Pizza Dough

Pizzeria Paradiso's bready and robust pizzas rise from this dough. Both crispy and chewy, it can star in a pizza of few toppings or perform the supporting role for your elaborately topped pie. While you can make this dough in an electric mixer (follow the method outlined in the whole wheat dough recipe on page 42), food processor, or bread machine, I have chosen to teach you the simple method of hand mixing using only your fingers and a dough scraper as your tools.

1) Mound the flour on a clean countertop and make a large well (about as wide as your out-stretched hand) in the center of the flour. Add the water and yeast to the well and let stand for 5 minutes to dissolve the yeast (**A**).

2) Using the index and middle fingers of one hand, mix the salt and oil into the water. Again using the index and middle fingers, gradually begin to draw the flour from the inside wall of the well into the water, being careful not to break the flour walls (**B**). Continue mixing the flour into the water until a loose dough is formed. Using a dough scraper, continue gradually mixing in the remaining flour until the dough forms a ball (**C**).

3) Using even pressure, begin kneading the ball of dough by pushing down and away with the heel of your hand (**D**). Next, take the far edge of the dough and fold it in half onto itself (**E**). Turn the dough a quarter turn. Push down and away again with the heel of your hand. Again fold the dough in half and turn. Continue kneading (pushing, folding, and turning), adding flour as necessary,

MAKES DOUGH FOR TWO 12-INCH (30 CM) PIZZAS

1 pound (455 g) white bread flour, plus more as needed

1 ¼ cups (285 ml) warm water

1 teaspoon active dry yeast

1 tablespoon (15 g) kosher salt

1 tablespoon (15 ml) olive oil

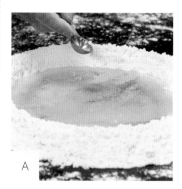

A

B

C

D

E

until the texture is smooth and springs back when you press the dough with your fingertip, or upward of 10 minutes. (See page 42.)

4) Place the dough in a bowl and cover it with plastic wrap. Let the dough rise until it has doubled in size, about 1 hour at room temperature or overnight in the refrigerator.

5) Turn the dough out onto a lightly floured work surface. Cut it into 2 equal pieces. Shape each piece into a ball. (See page 12.)

6) Place the dough balls on a floured plate and cover them with plastic wrap. Let them rise until doubled in size, about 1 hour at room temperature for room temperature dough or 2 to 3 hours at room temperature for cold dough. Or let rise in the refrigerator for 6 hours or up to overnight. (At this point, you may freeze the dough. When ready to use, thaw overnight in the refrigerator.) Allow refrigerated dough to stand at room temperature for 1 hour before using.

Winter Tomato Sauce

I call this "winter" tomato sauce because when tomatoes are out of season, you can still make this sauce and enjoy a bright tomato flavor. Uncooked and chunky, it has little in common with most tomato sauces. The chunks of tomato become both sauce and one of the pizza toppings. At Pizzeria Paradiso, we use a combination of diced canned tomatoes and crushed tomatoes; for the latter, we use Pomi brand.

1) Drain the diced tomatoes and place them in a large bowl (**A**).

2) Stir in the remaining ingredients.

3) Store the sauce in the refrigerator for up to 3 days or freeze for longer storage.

MAKES 2 ½ CUPS (565 G)

2 cups (484 g) canned diced tomatoes, drained (about one 28-ounce, or 800 g, can)

⅓ cup (60 g) canned crushed tomatoes

1 tablespoon (15 ml) olive oil

2 large fresh basil leaves torn into small pieces

1½ teaspoons chopped fresh Italian parsley

½ teaspoon kosher salt

Freshly ground black pepper to taste

A

The Paradiso

While we have 11 house pizzas with various combinations of toppings on Pizzeria Paradiso's menu, the Paradiso proudly sits at the top of the most frequently ordered pizza list. Many of our customers embellish this iconic tomato-and-cheese pizza, but we think it stands on its own: simple flavors perfectly married.

1) Cut the mozzarella into $\frac{1}{3}$-inch (about 1 cm) dice. You should have about $\frac{3}{4}$ cup (115 g).

2) Place a pizza stone on the top rack of a cool oven. Set the oven to broil and preheat for 30 minutes.

3) On a floured work surface, flatten the dough ball with your fingertips and stretch it into a 12-inch (30 cm) round. (See page 13.)

4) Sprinkle a pizza peel with cornmeal and lay the pizza dough round onto it. Spread the tomato sauce onto the pizza dough, leaving $\frac{1}{2}$ to $\frac{3}{4}$ inch (1.3 to 2 cm) of dough uncovered around the outside edge. Scatter the cheese on top of the tomato sauce. Sprinkle with salt and drizzle with oil.

5) Give the peel a quick shake to be sure the pizza is not sticking to the peel. Slide the pizza off the peel onto the stone in the oven. Broil for 1 minute and then turn the oven temperature to the highest bake setting and cook for 5 minutes. Quickly open the oven door, pull out the rack, and with a pair of tongs, rotate the pizza (not the stone) a half turn. Cook for 5 minutes more.

6) Using the peel, remove the pizza from the oven. Cut into slices and serve.

MAKES ONE 12-INCH (30 CM) PIZZA

4 ounces (115 g) fresh cow's milk mozzarella

1 ball Paradiso Pizza Dough

Cornmeal, for sprinkling

$\frac{3}{4}$ cup (170 g) Winter Tomato Sauce

Kosher salt to taste

Olive oil, for drizzling

Greg's Beer Cooler: Stout

The roasted malts in stouts really play well with the acid in the tomato sauce. Pick a stout with a moderate level of alcohol to cut the fat of the cheese.

Greg's Pick: North Coast Old Rasputin

THE PIZZARIA

Say "New York pizza" and the controversy begins: what qualifies as New York style, whose is best, what makes it special, and how to make it at home. Without making any undue claims, I think this dough can at least help to resolve the last part of the debate.

New York–Style Pizza Dough

Just like discussing pizza with a New Yorker, this dough tends to be sticky. Therefore, it may require a more liberal use of flour when shaping it into balls and when stretching it into pizza rounds. Because just a little too much water will make working with this dough much more difficult, I suggest weighing the water to ensure the accuracy of the amount added.

1) Place the water in the bowl of an electric mixer. Dissolve the yeast in the water and let stand for 5 minutes.

2) Whisk the salt, sugar, and oil into the water mixture.

3) Add the flour and place the bowl on the mixer. Using the dough hook attachment, mix on the lowest speed until a rough dough is formed **(A)**.

4) Raise the speed of the mixer to medium-high. Knead the dough until it clears the sides of the bowl, wraps itself around the hook, and has a smooth and elastic texture, 8 to 10 minutes **(B)**. The mixer may move about on the counter. Stabilize it by placing your hand on top of the mixer.

5) Cover the bowl with plastic wrap. Let the dough rise until doubled in size, about 1 hour at room temperature or overnight in the refrigerator.

6) Turn the dough out onto a generously floured work surface. Cut into 2 equal pieces. Dust your hands with flour and shape each piece into a ball. (See page 12.)

7) Place the dough balls on a floured plate and cover with plastic wrap. Let them rise until doubled in size, about 1 hour at room temperature for room temperature dough or 2 to 3 hours at room temperature for cold dough. Or let rise in the refrigerator for 6 hours or up to overnight. (At this point, you may freeze the dough. When ready to use, thaw overnight in the refrigerator.) Allow refrigerated dough to stand at room temperature for 1 hour before using.

MAKES DOUGH FOR
TWO 12-INCH (30 CM)
PIZZAS

12 ounces (by weight) (355 ml) warm water

1 ½ teaspoons active dry yeast

1 tablespoon (15 g) kosher salt

1 teaspoon sugar

2 tablespoons (28 ml) olive oil

1 pound (455 g) white bread flour

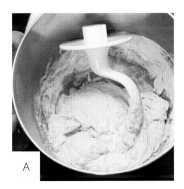

A

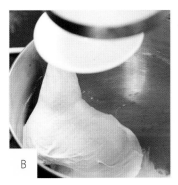

B

Slow-Cooked American Pizza Sauce

You can't have New York–Style pizza without oregano. Here you have my version of a slow-cooked American pizza sauce. I add a touch of sugar to cut the acid of the tomatoes and tease the palate.

1) Dice the tomatoes or crush them by hand into a large bowl.

2) Heat the olive oil in a large sauté pan over low heat until warm. Add the oregano and garlic and cook for a minute or two, until fragrant, stirring often to ensure that the garlic does not burn.

3) Add the tomatoes, onion, parsley, basil, sugar, salt, and several grindings of pepper. Raise the heat to medium-high. When the sauce begins to simmer, lower the heat and cook on low for about 1 hour. Remove from the heat and cool. Remove the onion pieces and the herb sprigs.

4) Place the mixture in a food processor and process for 30 seconds.

5) Store the sauce in the refrigerator for up to 3 days or freeze for longer storage.

MAKES 3 CUPS (680 G)

4 cups (960 g) canned whole tomatoes, drained (about two 28-ounce, or 800 g, cans)

3 tablespoons (45 ml) olive oil

2 teaspoons chopped fresh oregano

1 teaspoon chopped garlic

1 small onion, cut in half

3 sprigs fresh Italian parsley

1 sprig fresh basil

½ teaspoon sugar

½ teaspoon kosher salt

Freshly ground black pepper to taste

The Pizzaria

Pizzerias (often misspelled and known as pizz-ah-rias in the United States) dot the landscape of the American Northeast. This pie is my homage to them. Sprinkle each slice with some dried oregano and crushed red pepper flakes and you might feel transported to a corner pizza shop in Manhattan, New Haven, Boston, or Providence.

1) Place a pizza stone on the top rack of a cool oven. Set the oven to broil and preheat for 30 minutes.

2) On a generously floured work surface, flatten the dough ball with your fingertips and stretch it into a 12-inch (30 cm) round. (See page 13.)

3) Sprinkle a pizza peel with cornmeal and lay the pizza dough round on it. Spread the tomato sauce onto the pizza dough, leaving ½ to ¾ inch (1.3 to 2 cm) of dough uncovered around the outside edge. Scatter the cheese on top of the tomato sauce. Sprinkle with salt and drizzle with oil.

4) Give the peel a quick shake to be sure the pizza is not sticking to it. Slide the pizza off the peel onto the stone in the oven. Broil for 1 minute and then turn the oven temperature to the highest bake setting and cook for 5 minutes. Quickly open the oven door, pull out the rack, and with a pair of tongs, rotate the pizza (not the stone) a half turn. Cook for 5 minutes more.

5) Using the peel, remove the pizza from the oven. Cut into slices and serve.

MAKES ONE 12-INCH
(30 CM) PIZZA

1 ball New York–Style
Pizza Dough

Cornmeal, for sprinkling

¾ cup (170 g) Slow-Cooked
American Pizza Sauce

4 ounces (115 g) fresh cow's
milk mozzarella, shredded

Kosher salt to taste

Olive oil, for drizzling

THE NEAPOLITAN

In 1984, the Associazione Verace Pizza Napoletana (AVPN) established itself as the arbiter of "True Neapolitan" pizza. In 1998, the Italian government gave the AVPN's criteria for pizza its stamp of approval through a DOC (controlled designation of origin) classification. The recipe that follows reflects these standards.

Neapolitan-Style Pizza Dough

Plan ahead when making this soft and supple dough as it requires two slow rises. It will take at least 16, and up to 48, hours from beginning to end. I suggest making the dough in the morning of day one and serving the pizza for dinner the following day, with one rise at room temperature and the other in the refrigerator. Weigh the water for this recipe to ensure accuracy. You can order type "00" flour online if you find it hard to locate in local stores.

1) Place the water in the bowl of an electric mixer. Whisk the yeast into the water. Stir in 4 ounces (115 g) of the flour. Let stand for 1 hour (**A**).

2) In a separate bowl, mix together the remaining flour and the salt.

3) Place the bowl with the yeast mixture onto the mixer and fit with a paddle attachment. With the mixer on the lowest speed, add the flour and salt mixture slowly (¼ cup [31 g] at a time) until all of the flour is incorporated. Mix for about 2 minutes after each addition of flour.

4) Replace the paddle with the dough hook and knead the dough for 3 minutes on the lowest speed. Increase the speed to medium and continue kneading for 10 minutes or until the dough is smooth, elastic, and easily comes off the side of the bowl (**B**). Cover the bowl with plastic wrap and let the dough rise for 8 to 10 hours at room temperature or up to 24 hours in the refrigerator.

5) Turn the dough out onto a floured surface. Cut the dough into 2 equal pieces. Sprinkle each piece of dough with flour and lightly flour your hands. If your dough is tacky, use a generous amount of flour when shaping the balls of dough. Shape each piece into a ball. (See page 12.)

6) Place the dough balls on a floured plate and cover it with plastic wrap. Let rise for 6 to 8 hours at room temperature or up to 24 hours in the refrigerator, or until doubled in size. This is a soft dough that tends to spread when it rises. It may resemble a flattened ball at the completion of this rise. (At this point, you may freeze the dough. When ready to use, thaw overnight in the refrigerator.) Allow refrigerated dough to stand at room temperature for 1 hour before using.

MAKES DOUGH FOR
TWO 12-INCH (30 CM)
PIZZAS

12 ounces (355 ml) warm water

¼ teaspoon compressed
fresh yeast

1 pound (455 g) type "00" flour

1 tablespoon (19 g) sea
salt flakes, or 2 teaspoons
(11 g) Kosher salt

A

B

San Marzano Tomato Sauce

This simple sauce, good for any time of year, qualifies under the "True Neapolitan" pizza guidelines. You can also make this sauce with fresh tomatoes, but only the San Marzano tomato meets the DOC criteria. I like the freshness of this sauce since it cooks only once, in the oven, along with the dough it adorns.

MAKES 1 ½ CUPS (340 G)

2 cups (480 g) drained canned whole San Marzano tomatoes (about one 28-ounce, or 800 g, can)

½ teaspoon olive oil

¼ teaspoon sea salt flakes, or to taste

1) Pass the tomatoes through the medium blade of a food mill or a medium strainer into a mixing bowl. Stir in the olive oil and salt.

2) Store the sauce in the refrigerator for up to 3 days or freeze for longer storage.

The Neapolitan

The ingredients for this pie make it as close to a "True Neapolitan" pizza as you can get from your home oven. To fully qualify, you'd need a wood-burning oven with temperatures of 905° (485°C).

MAKES ONE 12-INCH (30 CM) PIZZA

1 ball Neapolitan-Style Pizza Dough

Cornmeal, for sprinkling

⅓ cup (75 g) San Marzano Tomato Sauce

3 ounces (85 g) fresh buffalo mozzarella, torn into 10 to 12 pieces

Sea salt flakes to taste

Olive oil, for drizzling

1) Place a pizza stone on the top rack of a cool oven. Set the oven to broil and preheat for 30 minutes.

2) On a floured counter, flatten the ball with your fingertips and stretch it into a 12-inch (30 cm) round. (See page 13.) If your dough is tacky, use a generous amount of flour when forming the pizza round.

3) Sprinkle a pizza peel with cornmeal and lay the pizza dough round on it. Spread the tomato sauce onto the pizza dough, leaving ½ to ¾ inch (1.3 to 2 cm) of dough uncovered around the outside edge. Arrange the cheese on top of the tomato sauce. Sprinkle with salt and drizzle with oil.

4) Give the peel a quick shake to be sure the pizza is not sticking to it. Slide the pizza off the peel onto the stone in the oven. Broil for 1 ½ minutes and then turn the oven temperature to the highest bake setting and cook for 4 minutes. Quickly open the oven door, pull out the rack, and with a pair of tongs, rotate the pizza (not the stone) a half turn. Cook for 4 to 5 minutes more.

5) Using the peel, remove the pizza from the oven. Cut into slices and serve.

THE GLUTEN-FREE

We didn't want our growing population of customers who are unable to digest gluten to have to live without Pizzeria Paradiso pizza, so we developed this dough and a robust roasted tomato sauce to go with it.

Gluten-Free Pizza Dough

You will note that everything changes when working with gluten-free dough, from the flour to the cooking method. Gluten is crucial to the structure of wheat-based pizza crust. In this recipe, the xanthan gum and eggs take over for the gluten. At Pizzeria Paradiso, we use Bob's Red Mill gluten-free flour. The resulting pizza crust bears a resemblance more akin to flatbread than to a traditional pizza crust.

1) Mix the baking flour, brown rice four, buckwheat flour, and xanthan gum together thoroughly in a medium bowl. Set aside.

2) Place the water in the bowl of an electric mixer. Dissolve the yeast in the water and let stand for 5 minutes.

3) Whisk the egg, egg yolk, and salt into the water mixture.

4) Add the flour mixture and place the bowl on the mixer. Using the paddle attachment, mix on the lowest speed until a rough dough is formed (**A**).

5) Scrape the dough onto the counter and shape it into a mound. Cut into 2 equal pieces. Shape each piece into a ¹/₂-inch-thick (1.3 cm) disk.

6) Sprinkle the counter with rice flour and roll the dough disk with a rolling pin into a 10-inch (28 cm) round.

7) Place the round of dough on a pizza peel dusted with rice flour (or a 10-inch or 25.5 cm round pan if freezing) and form a ¹/₂-inch (1.3 cm) lip around the edge of the pizza (**B**). After the lip is formed, the round will be closer to 9 inches (23 cm) in diameter. (At this point, you may freeze the dough. When ready to use, allow the dough to stand at room temperature for half an hour before using.)

MAKES TWO 9-INCH
(23 CM) PIZZAS

7 ½ ounces (215 g) gluten-free all-purpose baking flour

3 tablespoons each brown rice (30 g) and buckwheat (23 g) flours

1 ¾ teaspoons xanthan gum

½ cup plus 1 tablespoon (135 ml) warm water

2 teaspoons active dry yeast

1 large egg

1 egg yolk

1 teaspoon kosher salt

A

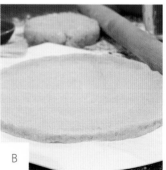

B

Roasted Tomato Sauce

Be forewarned: This sauce takes time. The rich, caramelized, deep tomato flavor that develops through the roasting process produces a sauce worth the wait. To roast the tomatoes correctly, scatter them in one layer with space between each piece. If the tomatoes do not have the space they need, they will stew rather than roast, and your sauce will not have the depth of flavor that proper roasting imparts. The water content of tomatoes can vary greatly. Since proper roasting depends on the evaporation of the tomato juices, check them every 15 minutes throughout the roasting process. Adjust the roasting time (more or less) based on the specific results you encounter.

1) Preheat the oven to 500°F (250°C, or gas mark 10).

2) Peel and seed the tomatoes. (See Fresh Tomato Sauce, page 43.) Cut the tomatoes into 1-inch (2.5 cm) pieces and place them in a large bowl. Toss with 3 tablespoons (45 ml) of the oil, $1/4$ teaspoon of the salt, and the pepper. Line two large roasting pans with aluminum foil or silicone baking liners. Scatter the tomatoes in a single layer in the pans. Roast in the oven for 30 to 45 minutes or until most of the moisture has evaporated and some pieces of tomato show significant browning **(A)**. Remove the tomatoes from the oven and cool. You should have just over $1 1/2$ cups (about 270 g) of roasted tomatoes.

3) Dice the pancetta into $1/4$-inch (6 mm) pieces. Heat the remaining olive oil in a sauté pan over medium heat until warm. Add the pancetta and cook until it has released some of its fat, about 5 minutes, stirring occasionally.

4) Add the onions and cook for several minutes or until soft. Turn the heat to low and add the garlic and thyme. Cook for several minutes more, stirring often to ensure the garlic does not burn.

5) Add the tomatoes, the remaining salt, and several grindings of pepper. Continue cooking for 5 to 10 minutes. Remove from the heat, add the basil and parsley, and cool.

6) Store the sauce in the refrigerator for up to 3 days or freeze for longer storage.

MAKES 1 ½ CUPS (340 G)

6 medium slicing tomatoes or 9 plum tomatoes

4 ½ tablespoons (68 ml) olive oil

½ teaspoon kosher salt

Freshly ground black pepper to taste

3 ounces (85 g) pancetta

¾ cup (120 g) chopped onion

1 ½ teaspoons finely chopped garlic

¾ teaspoon chopped fresh thyme

2 tablespoons (5 g) fresh basil chiffonade

1 tablespoon (4 g) coarsely chopped fresh Italian parsley

A

The Gluten-Free

Unlike traditional pizza dough, the gluten-free pizza will only develop small air pockets. I have chosen to use Pecorino Toscano cheese on this pie because the nutty character of the cheese highlights the nutty buckwheat flavors of the dough.

1) Place a pizza stone on the top rack of a cool oven. Set the oven to broil and preheat for 30 minutes.

2) Cut the cheese into $\frac{1}{3}$-inch (about 1 cm) dice. You should have about $\frac{1}{2}$ cup (70 g).

3) Brush the dough with olive oil. Spread the tomato sauce onto the pizza shell to the edge of the lip. Scatter the cheese over the tomato sauce. Sprinkle with salt and drizzle with oil.

4) Give the peel a quick shake to be sure the pizza is not sticking to it. Slide the pizza off the peel onto the stone in the oven. Broil for 1 minute and then turn to the highest bake setting and cook for 5 minutes. Quickly open the oven door, pull out the rack, and with a pair of tongs, rotate the pizza (not the stone) a half turn. Cook for 5 minutes more.

5) Using the peel, remove the pizza from the oven. Cut into slices and serve.

2 ½ ounces (70 g) Pecorino Toscano cheese (see page 21)

1 round Gluten-Free Pizza Dough

Rice flour, for sprinkling

Olive oil, for brushing and drizzling

½ cup plus 2 tablespoons (155 g) Roasted Tomato Sauce

Kosher salt to taste

THE WHOLE WHEAT

Pizza meets "health food" in this recipe, made with whole grains, fresh tomatoes, and vegan cheese.

Whole Wheat Pizza Dough

Using 100 percent whole wheat flour imparts a nutty flavor to this crispy, bready crust. If you like the heartiness of whole wheat bread, this dough, both flavorful and nutritious, will suit all your pizza needs.

1) Place the water in the bowl of an electric mixer. Dissolve the yeast in the water and let stand for 5 minutes.

2) Whisk the salt and oil into the water mixture.

3) Add the flour and place the bowl on the mixer. Using the dough hook attachment, mix on the lowest speed until a rough dough is formed **(A)**.

4) Raise the speed of the mixer slightly. Knead the dough until it has a smooth and elastic texture, about 5 minutes. To test the dough, turn off the machine and press the dough with your fingertip. When it begins to spring back, the dough is fully kneaded and ready to rise. Because this dough is made with 100 percent whole wheat flour, the dough may not spring back completely when pressed **(B)**.

5) Cover the bowl with plastic wrap. Let the dough rise until doubled in size, about 1 hour at room temperature or overnight in the refrigerator.

6) Turn the dough out onto a lightly floured work surface. Cut into 2 equal pieces. Shape each piece into a ball. (See page 12.)

7) Place the dough balls on a floured plate and cover with plastic wrap. Let them rise until doubled in size, about 1 hour at room temperature for room temperature dough or 2 to 3 hours at room temperature for cold dough. Or let rise in the refrigerator for 6 hours or up to overnight. (At this point, you may freeze the dough. When ready to use, thaw overnight in the refrigerator.) Allow refrigerated dough to stand at room temperature for 1 hour before using.

MAKES DOUGH FOR
TWO 12-INCH (30 CM)
PIZZAS

1 ½ cups (355 ml) warm water

1 teaspoon active dry yeast

1 tablespoon (15 g) kosher salt

1 tablespoon (15 ml) olive oil

1 pound (455 g) whole wheat flour

A

B

Fresh Tomato Sauce

Summer is tomato season and for me, those fresh, delicious tomatoes sing "pizza." When I'm not making a simple pie topped only with fresh sliced tomatoes, basil, and olive oil, I use the following sauce. The brightest, tastiest sauce comes from using tomatoes at the peak of tomato season. This sauce's simple method and quick cooking belie its depth of flavors.

1)   Bring a 4-quart (4 L) pot of water to a boil. Place the tomatoes, 2 or 3 at a time, in the boiling water for 30 seconds and then transfer them to a bowl of ice water. Working with one tomato at a time, score the skin with a paring knife. Lift a piece of the skin from the tomato flesh and begin peeling it away from the flesh. Continue peeling until all the skin has been removed. Repeat the process with the other tomatoes.

2)   Remove the core and cut each tomato in half horizontally. Working over a bowl, take a half of a tomato in your palm and squeeze gently and evenly against the flesh of the tomato until the seeds flow from the flesh. Repeat this with the other tomatoes. Discard the seeds **(A)**.

3)   Chop the tomato flesh into $1/2$-inch (1.3 cm) dice. You should have about 3 cups (about 540 g).

4)   Heat the olive oil in a large sauté pan over medium heat until warm. Add the garlic and oregano and cook for a minute or two until fragrant, stirring often to ensure the garlic does not burn.

5)   Add the tomatoes, parsley, salt, and several grindings of pepper. Cook until the tomatoes soften and begin to release their juices. Continue cooking for another minute. Remove from the heat and let cool.

6)   Store the sauce in the refrigerator for up to 3 days or freeze for longer storage.

MAKES 2 CUPS (450 G)

3–4 medium ripe tomatoes (about 1¾ pounds or 800 g)

3 tablespoons (45 ml) olive oil

1 tablespoon (10 g) chopped garlic

½ teaspoon chopped fresh oregano

1 tablespoon (4 g) chopped fresh Italian parsley

¾ teaspoon kosher salt

Freshly ground black pepper to taste

A

The Whole Wheat

Most of the pizzas in this book can be made vegan friendly by substituting soy-based or tapioca-based cheese substitutes. Of course, you can also use the whole wheat dough and the fresh tomato sauce in combination with dairy cheeses.

1) Place a pizza stone on the top rack of a cool oven. Set the oven to broil and preheat for 30 minutes.

2) On a generously floured work surface, flatten the dough ball with your fingertips and stretch it into a 12-inch (30 cm) round. (See page 13.)

3) Sprinkle a pizza peel with cornmeal and lay the pizza dough round on it. Spread the tomato sauce onto the pizza dough, leaving $1/2$ to $3/4$ inch (1.3 to 2 cm) of dough uncovered around the outside edge. Scatter the cheese on top of the tomato sauce. Sprinkle with salt and drizzle with oil.

4) Give the peel a quick shake to be sure the pizza is not sticking to the peel. Slide the pizza off the peel onto the stone in the oven. Broil for 1 minute. Turn the oven temperature to the highest bake setting and cook for 5 minutes. Quickly open the oven door, pull out the rack, and with a pair of tongs, rotate the pizza (not the stone) a half turn. Cook for 5 minutes more.

5) Using the peel, remove the pizza from the oven. Cut into slices and serve.

1 ball Whole Wheat
Pizza Dough

Cornmeal, for sprinkling

$3/4$ cup (170 g) Fresh
Tomato Sauce

4 ounces (115 g) vegan
mozzarella or regular
mozzarella, shredded or
diced ($3/4$ cup or 115 g)

Kosher salt, to taste

Olive oil, for drizzling

THE MULTIGRAIN

Complex flavors and textures develop in this pizza made with a dough of spent grain (a by-product of brewing beer), whole wheat flour, and white bread flour. You can ask your local craft brewer to save some spent grain for you, or try your hand at brewing beer if you feel adventurous.

Multigrain Pizza Dough

If you shy away from the spent grain, you can substitute other cooked grains, such as quinoa, spelt, barley, farro, or rice. Whatever grains you choose, pack them loosely when measuring.

1) Place the water in the bowl of an electric mixer. Dissolve the yeast in the water and let stand for 5 minutes.

2) Whisk the salt and oil into the water mixture.

3) Add the whole wheat and bread flours and place the bowl on the mixer. Using the dough hook attachment, mix on the lowest speed until a rough dough is formed.

4) Add the grain to the rough dough (**A**).

5) Raise the speed of the mixer to medium. Knead the dough until it has a smooth and elastic texture, about 5 minutes. To test the dough, turn off the machine and press the dough with your fingertip. When it begins to spring back, the dough is fully kneaded and ready to rise. Because this dough is made with a high ratio of whole wheat flour, the dough may not spring back completely when pressed.

6) Cover the bowl with plastic wrap. Let the dough rise until doubled in size, about 1 hour at room temperature or overnight in the refrigerator.

7) Turn the dough out onto a generously floured work surface. Cut into 2 equal pieces. Dust your hands with flour and shape each piece into a ball. (See page 12.)

8) Place the dough balls on a floured plate and cover with plastic wrap. Let them rise until doubled in size, about 1 hour at room temperature for room temperature dough or 2 to 3 hours at room temperature for cold dough. Or let rise in the refrigerator for 6 hours or up to overnight. (At this point, you may freeze the dough. When ready to use, thaw overnight in the refrigerator.) Allow refrigerated dough to stand at room temperature for 1 hour before using.

Note: Store spent grain in the freezer as its refrigerated shelf life is no more than a day or two.

MAKES DOUGH FOR
TWO 12-INCH (30 CM)
PIZZAS

1 ¼ cups (285 ml) warm water

1 teaspoon active dry yeast

1 tablespoon (15 g) kosher salt

2 tablespoons (28 ml) olive oil

10 ounces (280 g)
whole wheat flour

7 ounces (200 g) white
bread flour

¾ cup (about 165 g) loosely
packed spent grain (or other
cooked grain of your choice)

A

Spicy Tomato Sauce

Spicy, piccante, diavolo—there are many ways to say "hot" and many ways to make your sauce speak the language of heat. In this recipe, I use a moderate amount of two types of hot peppers. Please don't let the recipe inhibit you from adding more or less according to your taste or from substituting other pepper varieties.

1) Dice the canned tomatoes or crush them by hand into a large bowl (**A**).

2) Heat the olive oil in a large sauté pan over medium heat until warm. Add the onions and cook for several minutes or until soft.

3) Turn the heat to low and add the cherry peppers, garlic, thyme, and red pepper flakes. Cook for another minute or two until fragrant, stirring often to ensure the garlic does not burn.

4) Increase the heat to medium. Add the crushed tomatoes, sun-dried tomatoes, parsley, salt, and several grindings of pepper. Cook until the tomatoes soften and begin to release their juices. Continue to simmer for about 15 minutes to thicken the sauce and develop the flavor. Remove from the heat and cool.

5) Store the sauce in the refrigerator for up to 3 days or freeze for longer storage.

MAKES 3 CUPS
(675 G)

4 cups (960 g) drained canned whole tomatoes (about two 28-ounce, or 800 g, cans)

3 tablespoons (45 ml) olive oil

½ cup (80 g) chopped onion

1 tablespoon chopped pickled cherry peppers

1 teaspoon chopped garlic

¼ teaspoon chopped fresh thyme

¼ teaspoon crushed red pepper flakes

2 tablespoons (7 g) chopped sun-dried tomatoes

1 tablespoon (4 g) chopped fresh Italian parsley

1 teaspoon kosher salt

Freshly ground black pepper to taste

A

The Multigrain

"Substantial" aptly describes this pizza. The spent grain and whole wheat flour impart a robustness to the dough that combines with the piquancy of the sauce. They join together with the creamy fattiness of the cheese to deliver a unified whole of intricate flavors and intense satisfaction.

1) Place a pizza stone on the top rack of a cool oven. Set the oven to broil and preheat for 30 minutes.

2) Cut the cheese into ⅓-inch (about 1 cm) dice. You should have about ¾ cup (115 g).

3) On a generously floured work surface, flatten the dough ball with your fingertips and stretch it into a 12-inch (30 cm) round. (See page 13.)

4) Sprinkle a pizza peel with cornmeal and lay the pizza dough round on it. Spread the tomato sauce onto the pizza dough, leaving ½ to ¾ inch (1.3 to 2 cm) of dough uncovered around the outside edge. Sprinkle with salt and drizzle with oil.

5) Give the peel a quick shake to be sure the pizza is not sticking to the peel. Slide the pizza off the peel onto the stone in the oven. Broil for 1 minute. Turn the oven temperature to the highest bake setting and cook for 5 minutes. Quickly open the oven door, pull out the rack, and with a pair of tongs, rotate the pizza (not the stone) a half turn. Cook for 5 minutes more.

6) Using the peel, remove the pizza from the oven. Cut into slices and serve.

MAKES ONE 12-INCH (30 CM) PIZZA

4 ounces (115 g) Fontina cheese

1 ball Multigrain Pizza Dough

Cornmeal, for sprinkling

¾ cup (170 g) Spicy Tomato Sauce

Kosher salt to taste

Olive oil, for drizzling

Greg's Beer Cooler: Pale Ale

A pale ale's light malt sweetness balances and accentuates the spiciness of the tomato sauce here, and since you'll need more than one beer to quench your thirst, we picked a beer with a moderately low alcohol level.

Greg's Pick: DC Brau Public

THE DEEP DISH

Though this truly American pie has its detractors, it has no rivals.
Enjoy the taste of abundance in each mouthful.

Deep-Dish Pizza Dough

I make no claims that you will feel the wind off Lake Michigan or hear the rat-a-tat of a mobster's machine gun when you eat pizza made from this dough. What I will claim is that the dough will make a classic Chicago-style, biscuit-textured, buttery crust.

1) Place the water in the bowl of an electric mixer. Dissolve the yeast in the water and let stand for 5 minutes.

2) Whisk the salt, sugar, oil, and butter into the water mixture.

3) Add the flour and place the bowl on the mixer. Using the dough hook attachment, mix on the lowest speed until a rough dough is formed **(A)**.

4) Raise the speed of the mixer slightly and knead the dough for 2 to 3 minutes. You do not want to overwork the dough. The dough will come together in a ball, but it will not be as smooth and elastic as most pizza and bread doughs.

5) Cover the bowl with plastic wrap and let the dough rise for 2 hours at room temperature.

6) Place the dough on a floured counter and cut into 2 equal pieces. (At this point, you may freeze the dough. When ready to use, thaw overnight in the refrigerator. Allow the dough to stand at room temperature for 1 hour before using.)

MAKES DOUGH FOR TWO 10-INCH (25.5 CM) PIZZAS

1¼ (285 ml) cups warm water

2¾ teaspoons (11 g) active dry yeast

1 tablespoon (15 g) kosher salt

1¼ teaspoons sugar

¼ cup plus 2 tablespoons (90 ml) olive oil

2½ tablespoons (35 g) butter, melted

1¼ pounds (570 g) all-purpose flour

Quick-Cooked Tomato Sauce

This sauce lives up to its name, cooking in only about 10 minutes. Perfect for a long-cooking deep-dish pie, it develops its full flavor as the pie cooks in the oven.

1) Dice the tomatoes or crush them by hand into a large bowl.

2) Heat the olive oil in a large sauté pan over low heat until warm. Add the garlic and oregano and cook for a minute or two until fragrant, stirring often to ensure the garlic does not burn.

3) Add the tomatoes, parsley, salt, and several grindings of pepper. Increase the heat to high and cook until the tomatoes soften and begin to release their juices. Cook for 2 to 3 minutes more, stirring occasionally, until the sauce is juicy while still retaining distinct chunks of tomato. Remove from the heat and cool **(B)**.

4) Store the sauce in the refrigerator for up to 3 days or freeze for longer storage.

MAKES 2 ½ CUPS (565 G)

4 cups (960 g) drained canned whole tomatoes (about two 28-ounce, or 800 g, cans)

3 tablespoons (45 ml) olive oil

1 tablespoon (10 g) chopped garlic

½ teaspoon chopped fresh oregano

1 tablespoon (4 g) chopped fresh Italian parsley

1 teaspoon kosher salt

Freshly ground black pepper to taste

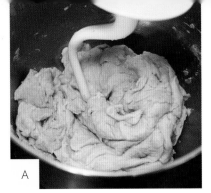
A

B

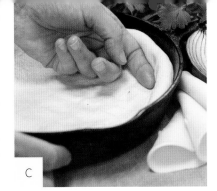
C

The Deep Dish

With an abundance of cheese, deep tomato flavors, and a substantial crust, the Deep Dish satisfies a hearty Midwestern appetite.

1) Position a rack in the middle of the oven. Preheat the oven to the highest bake setting.

2) Brush a 10-inch (25.5 cm) cast iron skillet or cake pan with olive oil. Using your fingertips, flatten the dough into a ¹/₂-inch-thick (1.3 cm) round. Lay the dough into the prepared skillet. Press the dough with your fingertips. Then use the back of your finger to press the dough until it covers the bottom of the skillet and reaches about 1 inch (2.5 cm) up the side of the skillet **(C)**.

3) Arrange the mozzarella and provolone cheeses on top of the dough. Scatter the parsley, basil, and oregano over the cheese. Spread the tomato sauce over the herbs. Sprinkle with the Parmesan cheese and salt and drizzle with oil.

4) Place the pie on the middle rack of your oven. Turn the oven temperature to 450°F (230°C or gas mark 8) and bake for 30 to 35 minutes until the crust is golden brown and the tomato and cheese are bubbling.

5) Remove the pizza from the oven, cut into slices, and serve.

MAKES ONE
10-INCH (25.5 CM)
DEEP-DISH PIZZA

Olive oil, for brushing and drizzling

1 piece Deep-Dish Pizza Dough

5 ounces (140 g) cow's milk mozzarella, sliced

4 ounces (115 g) provolone cheese, sliced

1 teaspoon roughly chopped fresh Italian parsley

1 teaspoon fresh basil chiffonade

¼ teaspoon finely chopped fresh oregano

1¼ cups (280 g) Quick-Cooked Tomato Sauce

2 tablespoons (10 g) finely grated Parmesan cheese

Kosher salt, to taste

THE CLASSICS

As we move on from the basic tomato-and-cheese pizzas, we turn to Italy, the birthplace of modern pizza, for seven traditional selections. The pizzas in this section represent the most well-known Italian pizzas. Of course, the thing about pizza is that it adapts to the tastes of the *pizzaiolo*, or pizza maker. Thus, most of these recognizable standards vary widely from pizzeria to pizzeria. The overarching sensibility is simplicity. A few flavors or toppings grace a delicate yet chewy crust.

In these recipes, we traverse the country to enjoy its bounty, from the olives of Apulia and the anchovies of Naples to the pecorino cheese of Tuscany, the prosciutto di Parma of Emilia-Romagna, and the Gorgonzola of Piedmont. Taken together, the recipes will guide you through the enchanting flavors of Italy. Use high-quality ingredients and don't forget the olive oil and you will enjoy your travels.

Net Wt: 1 Kg (2.2 lb.)

PIZZA MARGHERITA

The classic. The myth. The prototype. Did the world's love affair with pizza begin
with Queen Margherita and the colors of the Italian flag? According to legend,
Raffaele Esposito, a Neapolitan pizzaiolo, made the first tomato, basil, and mozzarella
pizza in 1889 for Queen Margherita of Savoy. We may never know the veracity
of the legend, but thankfully with this recipe we can take a bite of the story.

1) Place a pizza stone on the top rack of a cool oven. Set the oven to broil and preheat for 30 minutes.

2) On a generously floured counter, flatten the dough ball with your fingertips and stretch it into a 12-inch (30 cm) round. (See page 13.)

3) Sprinkle a pizza peel with cornmeal and lay the pizza dough round on it. Spread the tomato sauce onto the pizza dough, leaving 1/2 to 3/4 inch (1.3 to 2 cm) of dough uncovered around the outside edge. Place the basil leaves evenly around the pizza. Arrange the cheese on top of the sauce and basil. Sprinkle with salt and drizzle with oil **(A)**.

4) Give the peel a quick shake to be sure the pizza is not sticking to the peel. Slide the pizza off the peel onto the stone in the oven. Broil for 1 1/2 minutes. Turn the oven temperature to the highest bake setting and cook for 4 minutes. Quickly open the oven door, pull out the rack, and with a pair of tongs, rotate the pizza (not the stone) a half turn. Cook for 4 to 5 minutes more.

5) Using the peel, remove the pizza from the oven. Cut into slices and serve.

Note: Add the basil as the recipe indicates or, for a brighter basil taste, add a chiffonade of basil when the pizza emerges from the oven.

MAKES ONE 12-INCH
(30 CM) PIZZA

1 ball Neapolitan-Style
Pizza Dough (page 35)

Cornmeal, for sprinkling

1/3 cup (75 g) San Marzano
Tomato Sauce (page 36)

8 to 10 large basil
leaves, torn in half

3 ounces (85 g) fresh
buffalo mozzarella, torn
into 10 to 12 pieces

Sea salt flakes, to taste

Olive oil, for drizzling

A

LEVEL 2: THE CLASSICS ❀ 55

PIZZA MARINARA

Pizza Margherita and Pizza Marinara represent two of the three formally recognized "True Neapolitan" pizzas. While officially pizza, this could also be referred to as tomato bread. One bite of this simple crust of bread, graced only with crushed tomatoes, fresh oregano, sliced garlic, and extra-virgin olive oil, and you might swear you can taste the salt air of Naples.

1) Place a pizza stone on the top rack of a cool oven. Set the oven to broil and preheat for 30 minutes.

2) On a generously floured work surface, flatten the dough ball with your fingertips and stretch it into a 12-inch (30 cm) round. (See page 13.)

3) Sprinkle a pizza peel with cornmeal and lay the pizza dough round on it. Spread the tomato sauce onto the pizza dough, leaving ½ to ¾ inch (1.3 to 2 cm) of dough uncovered around the outside edge. Scatter the garlic and sprinkle the oregano on top of the tomato sauce **(A)**. Sprinkle the pizza with salt and drizzle with olive oil.

4) Give the peel a quick shake to be sure the pizza is not sticking to the peel. Slide the pizza off the peel onto the stone in the oven. Broil for 1 minute and then turn the oven temperature to the highest bake setting and cook for 5 minutes. Quickly open the oven door, pull out the rack, and with a pair of tongs, rotate the pizza (not the stone) a half turn. Cook for 5 minutes more.

5) Using the peel, remove the pizza from the oven. Drizzle with oil. Cut into slices and serve.

MAKES ONE 12-INCH
(30 CM) PIZZA

1 ball Neapolitan–Style
Pizza Dough (page 35)

Cornmeal, for sprinkling

⅓ cup (75 g) San Marzano
Tomato Sauce (page 36)

1 tablespoon (10 g) very
thinly sliced garlic

1 teaspoon chopped
fresh oregano

Kosher salt, to taste

Olive oil, for drizzling

A

PIZZA QUATTRO FORMAGGI

In the classic pizza quattro formaggi, four cheeses meld to create a rich, decadent pizza that satisfies the heartiest of appetites. You can choose the cheeses below or substitute others to suit your taste. A touch of garlic balances the richness. At Pizzeria Paradiso and in this recipe, we add a fifth cheese—Parmesan—for a bit of muskiness and salt. Thus making this recipe a Pizza Cinque Formaggi.

1) Place a pizza stone on the top rack of a cool oven. Set the oven to broil and preheat for 30 minutes.

2) Cut the mozzarella, pecorino, and Fontina cheeses into ⅓-inch (about 1 cm) dice. You should have just over 1 cup (141 g) combined.

3) On a floured work surface, flatten the dough ball with your fingertips and stretch it into a 12-inch (30 cm) round. (See page 13.)

4) Sprinkle a pizza peel with cornmeal and lay the pizza dough round on it. Using two spoons, dot the dough evenly with the Gorgonzola. Scatter the diced cheeses on top of the dough, leaving ½ to ¾ inch (1.3 to 2 cm) of dough uncovered around the outside edge. Sprinkle with 1 tablespoon (5 g) of the Parmesan. Scatter the garlic over the cheeses. Sprinkle with the parsley and salt (A).

5) Give the peel a quick shake to be sure the pizza is not sticking to the peel. Slide the pizza off the peel onto the stone in the oven. Broil for 1 minute. Turn the oven temperature to the highest bake setting and cook for 5 minutes. Quickly open the oven door, pull out the rack, and with a pair of tongs, rotate the pizza (not the stone) a half turn. Cook for 3 minutes more.

6) Using the peel, remove the pizza from the oven. Sprinkle with the remaining Parmesan cheese. Cut into slices and serve.

MAKES ONE 12-INCH (30 CM) PIZZA

3 ounces (85 g) fresh cow's milk mozzarella

1 ounce (28 g) Pecorino Toscano cheese (see page 21)

1 ounce (28 g) Fontina cheese

1 ball Neapolitan–Style or Paradiso Pizza Dough (page 35 or 27)

Cornmeal, for sprinkling

2 ounces (55 g) Gorgonzola cheese

2 tablespoons (10 g) freshly grated Parmesan cheese

1 teaspoon chopped garlic

1 tablespoon (4 g) chopped fresh Italian parsley

Kosher salt, to taste

A

Greg's Beer Cooler: Barrel–Aged Sour Ale

If you love red wine and blue cheese, try this match. The sweet and funky notes in the Gorgonzola have a natural affinity for the wild flora flavoring these sour ales.

Greg's Pick: BFM Abbaye de Saint Bon-Chien

PIZZA DI PROSCIUTTO

Prosciutto di Parma adorns pizzas across Italy. I chose the classic Italian combination of figs and prosciutto to represent this tradition. I made it even more decadently delicious by sweetening it with caramelized onions and fattening it up with Gorgonzola cheese. The rich mahogany color heralds a luscious depth of flavor brightened by highlights of sliced pink prosciutto. All I can say is, "Enjoy!"

A

B

C

1) Melt the butter in a large sauté pan over medium-low heat. Add the onions to the pan and stir to coat. Stir in the rosemary and salt **(A)** and cover the pan. Cook for 10 to 15 minutes or until the onions have released some liquid and are soft. Remove the lid and continue cooking. Once the liquid has evaporated, the onions will begin to brown. Stir the onions every few minutes for 30 to 45 minutes until they brown to a deep caramel color but do not burn. Remove from the heat and cool **(B)**. You should have about ¾ cup (115 g).

2) Meanwhile, place a pizza stone on the top rack of a cool oven. Set the oven to broil and preheat for 30 minutes.

3) On a floured work surface, flatten the dough ball with your fingertips and stretch it into a 12-inch (30 cm) round. (See page 13.)

4) Sprinkle a pizza peel with cornmeal and lay the pizza dough round on it. Using two spoons or your fingers, dot the dough evenly with the Gorgonzola, leaving ½ to ¾ inch (1.3 to 2 cm) of dough uncovered around the outside edge. Scatter the caramelized onions around the dough. Place the figs evenly over the onions **(C)**. Sprinkle with salt.

5) Give the peel a quick shake to be sure the pizza is not sticking to the peel. Slide the pizza off the peel onto the stone in the oven. Broil for 1 minute. Turn the oven temperature to the highest bake setting and cook for 5 minutes. Quickly open the oven door, pull out the rack, and with a pair of tongs, rotate the pizza (not the stone) a half turn. Cook for 5 minutes more.

6) Using the peel, remove the pizza from the oven. Tear the prosciutto slices into wide strips and lay them over the top of the pizza. Cut into slices and serve.

Note: If fresh figs are unavailable, you can replace them with dried figs. Heat ½ cup (120 ml) fruity red wine in a saucepan to just below a boil and remove from heat. Add the figs to the wine and soak for about 10 minutes; then drain and proceed.

MAKES ONE 12-INCH
(30 CM) PIZZA

3 tablespoons (42 g) butter

1½ medium onions, peeled and sliced

1 teaspoon finely chopped fresh rosemary

½ teaspoon kosher salt

1 ball Neapolitan–Style or Paradiso Pizza Dough (page 35 or 27)

Cornmeal, for sprinkling

4 ounces (115 g) Gorgonzola cheese

5 fresh figs (see Note), quartered

Kosher salt, to taste

3 very thin slices prosciutto di Parma

CALZONE

The folded pizza, or calzone, comes in as many varieties as pizza itself, with three ingredients—tomato, ham, and ricotta—appearing regularly. When making dough for calzones, divide the dough into three equal portions and then shape them into balls. The smaller-size dough ball, and resulting calzone, will help ensure thorough cooking.

A

B

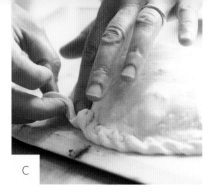
C

1) Place a pizza stone on the top rack of a cool oven. Set the oven to broil and preheat for 30 minutes.

2) Season the ricotta with salt and pepper.

3) On a floured work surface, flatten the dough ball with your fingertips and stretch it into a 9-inch (23 cm) round. (See page 13.)

4) Sprinkle a pizza peel with cornmeal and lay the pizza dough round on it. Spread half of the ricotta cheese onto the bottom half of the pizza dough, leaving $1/2$ to $3/4$ inch (1.3 to 2 cm) of dough uncovered around the outside edge. Spoon $1/4$ cup (58 g) of the tomato sauce over the cheese. Arrange the spinach and prosciutto slices on top of the sauce. Dot the remaining ricotta over the spinach and prosciutto. Sprinkle with the oregano and salt. Drizzle with oil **(A)**.

5) Fold the untopped half of the dough over the topped half. Press the edges of the dough together. Place the tip of your index finger at the top edge of the dough, and twist the edge of the dough over your fingertip **(B)**. Move your finger just past the twist and twist again. Continue along the edge of the calzone until the entire edge has been crimped **(C)**. Drizzle the top of the calzone with oil.

6) Give the peel a quick shake to be sure the calzone is not sticking to the peel. Slide the calzone off the peel onto the stone in the oven. Broil for 1 minute. Turn the oven temperature to the highest bake setting and cook for 5 minutes. Quickly open the oven door, pull out the rack, and with a pair of tongs, rotate the calzone (not the stone) a half turn. Cook for 5 minutes more. Meanwhile, in a small pot, warm the remaining tomato sauce.

7) Using the peel, remove the calzone from the oven. Cut in half and serve with the warm tomato sauce on the side.

MAKES ONE 9-INCH
(23 CM) CALZONE

$1/2$ cup (125 g) whole-milk ricotta cheese

Kosher salt, to taste

Freshly ground black pepper, to taste

1 small ball Neapolitan–Style or Paradiso Pizza Dough (page 35 or 27)

Cornmeal, for sprinkling

$1/2$ cup (115 g) tomato sauce of your choice

1⅓ cups (40 g) baby spinach leaves

3 very thin slices prosciutto di Parma

$1/2$ teaspoon chopped fresh oregano

Olive oil, for drizzling

PIZZA QUATTRO STAGIONI

Each quarter of this pizza represents a culinary season of the year. Artichokes are for spring, basil is for summer, mushrooms are for fall, and olives are for winter. In today's world, when seasonality is all but irrelevant, this traditional pizza reminds us of a time when food trends revolved around the sun.

1) Place a pizza stone on the top rack of a cool oven. Set the oven to broil and preheat for 30 minutes.

2) Cut the mozzarella into ⅓-inch (about 1 cm) dice. You should have about ¾ cup (115 g).

3) On a floured work surface, flatten the dough ball with your fingertips and stretch it into a 12-inch (30 cm) round. (See page 13.)

4) Sprinkle a pizza peel with cornmeal and lay the pizza dough round on it. Spread the tomato sauce onto the pizza dough, leaving ½ to ¾ inch (1.3 to 2 cm) of dough uncovered around the outside edge. Scatter the cheese on top of the sauce.

5) Imagine the pizza divided into four sections. Place the mushrooms on top of the cheese on one quarter of the pizza, the artichokes on the second quarter, the olives on the third section, and finally the basil on the fourth quarter **(A)**. Sprinkle the entire pizza with salt and drizzle with oil.

6) Give the peel a quick shake to be sure the pizza is not sticking to the peel. Slide the pizza off the peel onto the stone in the oven. Broil for 1 minute. Turn the oven temperature to the highest bake setting and cook for 5 minutes. Quickly open the oven door, pull out the rack, and with a pair of tongs, rotate the pizza (not the stone) a half turn. Cook for 5 minutes more.

7) Using the peel, remove the pizza from the oven. Cut into slices and serve.

Note: When possible, use cooked fresh artichoke hearts, sliced or quartered, or baby artichoke quarters. If you cannot find fresh artichokes, substitute canned, jarred (not marinated), or frozen hearts or quarters. At Pizzeria Paradiso, we use frozen baby artichoke quarters and roast and marinate them ourselves before using them on pizzas and salads.

A

MAKES ONE 12-INCH (30 CM) PIZZA

4 ounces (115 g) fresh cow's milk mozzarella

1 ball Neapolitan–Style or Paradiso Pizza Dough (page 35 or 27)

Cornmeal, for sprinkling

⅓ cup (75 g) San Marzano Tomato Sauce (page 36)

1 or 2 cremini mushrooms, thinly sliced

5 to 7 artichoke pieces (see Note)

3 to 6 Cerignola or Kalamata olives, pitted and coarsely chopped (see page 23)

3 or 4 large fresh basil leaves, torn in half

Kosher salt, to taste

Olive oil, for drizzling

PIZZA NAPOLETANA

This classic pizza has held a place on the Pizzeria Paradiso menu since we opened. Though the anchovies scare away some customers, it remains one of my favorites due to its bold, piquant flavors of anchovies and capers.

1) Place a pizza stone on the top rack of a cool oven. Set the oven to broil and preheat for 30 minutes.

2) Cut the mozzarella into ⅓-inch (about 1 cm) dice. You should have about ¾ cup (140 g).

3) On a floured work surface, flatten the dough ball with your fingertips and stretch it into a 12-inch (30 cm) round. (See page 13.)

4) Sprinkle a pizza peel with cornmeal and lay the pizza dough round on it. Spread the tomato sauce onto the pizza dough, leaving ½ to ¾ inch (1.3 to 2 cm) of dough uncovered around the outside edge. Scatter the capers and garlic and sprinkle the parsley and oregano on top of the tomato sauce. Place the anchovies evenly around the pizza **(A)**. Scatter the cheese on top of the pizza. Sprinkle with salt and drizzle with oil.

5) Give the peel a quick shake to be sure the pizza is not sticking to the peel. Slide the pizza off the peel onto the stone in the oven. Broil for 1 minute. Turn the oven temperature to the highest bake setting and cook for 5 minutes. Quickly open the oven door, pull out the rack, and with a pair of tongs, rotate the pizza (not the stone) a half turn. Cook for 5 minutes more.

6) Using the peel, remove the pizza from the oven. Cut into slices and serve.

A

MAKES ONE 12-INCH (30 CM) PIZZA

5 ounces (140 g) fresh cow's milk mozzarella

1 ball Neapolitan–Style or Paradiso Pizza Dough (page 35 or 27)

Cornmeal, for sprinkling

½ cup (115 g) San Marzano Tomato Sauce (page 36)

2 tablespoons (17 g) capers

1 teaspoon chopped garlic

1 tablespoon (4 g) chopped fresh Italian parsley

1 teaspoon chopped fresh oregano

1 heaping tablespoon (15 g) anchovy fillets (4 or 5 fillets)

Kosher salt, to taste

Olive oil, for drizzling

Greg's Beer Cooler: Lager

This pizza is like a salt bomb, so you want a beer you can throw back to quench your thirst. Lagers (or pilsners) fill the bill, since they're effervescent, clean, crisp, and quaffable.
Greg's Pick: Augustiner-Bräu München Edelstoff

PIZZERIA PARADISO ORIGINALS

This chapter invites you to don an apron and become a Pizzeria Paradiso *pizzaiolo*. The seven Pizzeria Paradiso standard pizzas that follow start with a crispy, bready crust topped with chunky tomatoes and a variety of toppings.

While you will recognize most of the toppings, you will also find a few that might surprise you. To start with the familiar, try the Macellaio, also known as the Pizzeria Paradiso meat lover's pizza, or the Siciliana, the veggie lover's pizza.

When you're ready, venture into more unfamiliar territory. Never had potatoes on a pizza? Intrigued by an egg cracked over a pizza and baked right along with it? These novel and fun toppings, plus mussels baked in their shell atop your pizza, await you in the pages ahead.

We follow the Italian model at Pizzeria Paradiso, adorning the crust lightly with the very best-quality toppings, drizzling them with olive oil, and letting the whole exceed the sum of its parts.

PIZZA MACELLAIO

With this pizza, Pizzeria Paradiso tips its hat to the meat lover. In the recipe that follows, we introduce the macellaio (butcher) to the birraio (brewer), paying homage to the classic combination of pizza and beer. We make our own spicy, garlicky pork sausage at Pizzeria Paradiso. You can purchase a prepared sausage you enjoy. Or, to make your own, ask your macellaio to coarsely grind pork shoulder. At home, add herbs and spices to your taste.

1) Place a pizza stone on the top rack of a cool oven. Set the oven to broil and preheat for 30 minutes.

2) Cut the mozzarella into ⅓-inch (about 1 cm) dice. You should have about ¾ cup (115 g).

3) On a generously floured work surface, flatten the dough ball with your fingertips and stretch it into a 12-inch (30 cm) round. (See page 13.)

4) Sprinkle a pizza peel with cornmeal and lay the pizza dough round on it. Spread the tomato sauce onto the pizza dough, leaving ½ to ¾ inch (1.2 to 2 cm) of dough uncovered around the outside edge. Arrange the pepperoni on top of the tomato sauce. Scatter the cheese on top of the pepperoni. Arrange the sausage and red onion rings on top of the cheese. Sprinkle with salt and drizzle with oil.

5) Give the peel a quick shake to be sure the pizza is not sticking to the peel. Slide the pizza off the peel onto the stone in the oven. Broil for 1 minute. Turn the oven temperature to the highest bake setting and cook for 5 minutes. Quickly open the oven door, pull out the rack, and with a pair of tongs rotate the pizza (not the stone) a half turn. Cook for 5 minutes more. Using the peel, remove the pizza from the oven. Cut into slices and serve.

MAKES ONE
12-INCH (30 CM)
PIZZA

4 ounces (115 g) fresh cow's milk mozzarella

1 ball Multigrain Pizza Dough (page 46)

Cornmeal, for sprinkling

¾ cup (170 g) Birreria Tomato Sauce

1 ounce (28 g) pepperoni, thinly sliced

2 ½ ounces (70 g) bulk pork sausage

5 very thin slices red onion

Kosher salt, to taste

Olive oil, for drizzling

Birreria Tomato Sauce

1) Heat the olive oil in a large sauté pan over medium heat until warm. Add the onions and cook for several minutes or until soft.

2) Turn the heat to low. Add the garlic and thyme and cook for a minute or two until fragrant, stirring often to ensure the garlic does not burn.

3) Add the tomatoes, beer, salt, and several grindings of pepper. Simmer for about 1 hour. Remove from the heat and cool.

4) Store the sauce in the refrigerator for up to 3 days or freeze for longer storage.

MAKES 2 ¼ CUPS
(505 G)

3 tablespoons (45 ml) olive oil

2 cups (320 g) chopped onion

2 teaspoons chopped garlic

2 teaspoons chopped fresh thyme

3 cups (540 g) canned crushed tomatoes, drained (about one 28-ounce, or 800 g, can)

½ cup (120 ml) porter or stout beer of your choice

½ teaspoon kosher salt

Freshly ground black pepper to taste

Greg's Beer Cooler: Smoked Porter

Like Sonny completes Cher, the porter's subtle smokiness combines with the meaty, savory flavors of the pepperoni and sausage, while the roasted malt and tomato dance in unison like Fred and Ginger.

Greg's Pick: Stone Smoked Porter

PIZZA BOSCO

A Pizzeria Paradiso favorite, Pizza Bosco boasts a triumvirate of favorite pizza toppings: mushrooms, spinach, and onion. The three combine to give a robust, earthy flavor to the pizza that calls to mind the forest or woods of its name, *bosco*.

1) Place a pizza stone on the top rack of a cool oven. Set the oven to broil and preheat for 30 minutes.

2) Cut the mozzarella into ⅓-inch (about 1 cm) dice. You should have about ¾ cup (115 g).

3) On a floured work surface, flatten the dough ball with your fingertips and stretch it into a 12-inch (30 cm) round. (See page 13.)

4) Sprinkle a pizza peel with cornmeal and lay the pizza dough round on it. Spread the tomato sauce onto the pizza dough, leaving ½ to ¾ inch (1.3 to 2 cm) of dough uncovered around the outside edge. Place the spinach leaves on top of the sauce (**A**). Scatter the cheese over the spinach and sauce. Arrange the mushrooms and rings of onion evenly on top of the cheese. Sprinkle with salt and drizzle with oil.

5) Give the peel a quick shake to be sure the pizza is not sticking to the peel. Slide the pizza off the peel onto the stone in the oven. Broil for 1 minute. Turn the oven temperature to the highest bake setting and cook for 5 minutes. Quickly open the oven door, pull out the rack, and with a pair of tongs, rotate the pizza (not the stone) a half turn. Cook for 5 minutes more.

6) Using the peel, remove the pizza from the oven. Cut into slices and serve.

A

MAKES ONE 12-INCH (30 CM) PIZZA

4 ounces (115 g) fresh cow's milk mozzarella

1 ball Paradiso Pizza Dough (page 27)

Cornmeal, for sprinkling

¾ cup (170 g) Winter Tomato Sauce (page 28)

2 cups (60 g) loosely packed baby spinach leaves

1 ounce (28 g) portabella mushrooms, very thinly sliced

5 very thin slices red onion

Kosher salt, to taste

Olive oil, for drizzling

Greg's Beer Cooler: Belgian Pale Ale

Belgian pale ales generally pair well with vegetables. In this case, the earthy notes of the BPA enrich the simple, bucolic flavors of spinach and mushrooms, refining the rustic and adding elegance to the pastoral.

Greg's Pick: Brasserie de la Senne Taras Boulba

PIZZA DI MARE

Imagine a bowl of sweet, garlicky mussels ladled atop a slice of rustic bread. Then imagine picking that up with your fingers and taking a big bite. This pizza makes that dream come true. The mussels will release their juices as the pizza bakes, resulting in a moist center and a nod to that bowl of your dreams. Remember to discard any chipped, cracked, or open mussels, as they may not be fresh and could turn your dream into a nightmare.

1) Place a pizza stone on the top rack of a cool oven. Set the oven to broil and preheat for 30 minutes.

2) Scrub the mussel shells with a stiff brush. Remove and discard the beards of the mussels **(A)**.

A

3) On a floured work surface, flatten the dough ball with your fingertips and stretch it into a 12-inch (30 cm) round. (See page 13.)

4) Sprinkle a pizza peel with cornmeal and lay the pizza dough round on it. Spread the tomato sauce onto the pizza dough, leaving $1/2$ to $3/4$ inch (1.3 to 2 cm) of dough uncovered around the outside edge. Scatter the garlic and sprinkle the parsley on top of the tomato sauce. Sprinkle with $1/4$ cup (25 g) of the Parmesan cheese and salt. Place the mussels evenly around the pizza **(B)**. Drizzle with oil.

B

5) Give the peel a quick shake to be sure the pizza is not sticking to the peel. Slide the pizza off the peel onto the stone in the oven. Broil for 1 minute. Turn the oven temperature to the highest bake setting and cook for 5 minutes. Quickly open the oven door, pull out the rack, and with a pair of tongs, rotate the pizza (not the stone) a half turn. Cook for 5 minutes more.

6) Using the peel, remove the pizza from the oven. Sprinkle with the remaining Parmesan cheese. Cut into slices and serve.

Greg's Beer Cooler: Belgian Strong Golden Ale

Dine like a Belgian with *moules* and *bier*. A clean, bright, and crisp Belgian Strong Golden Ale juxtaposes against the brackish brine of the sea.

Greg's Pick: Duvel Moortgat

MAKES ONE 12-INCH (30 CM) PIZZA

10 fresh mussels in the shell

1 ball Paradiso Pizza Dough (page 27)

Cornmeal, for sprinkling

$3/4$ cup (170 g) Winter Tomato Sauce (page 28)

1 teaspoon chopped garlic

2 teaspoons chopped fresh Italian parsley

$1/4$ cup plus 1 tablespoon (30 g) freshly grated Parmesan cheese

Kosher salt, to taste

Olive oil, for drizzling

PIZZA SICILIANA

Welcome to the Pizzeria Paradiso veggie lover's pizza, named for the combination of vegetables that remind us of the classic Sicilian dish *caponata*. At the restaurant, we use salt-preserved capers (flower buds of the caper plant), which must be rinsed and soaked before using (see page 23). Capers are also readily available pickled in a vinegar brine. You may use either when making this Southern Italian classic.

A

1) Place a pizza stone on the top rack of a cool oven. Set the oven to broil and preheat for 30 minutes.

2) Cut the mozzarella and pecorino into $\frac{1}{3}$-inch (about 1 cm) dice. You should have about $\frac{3}{4}$ (110 g) cup cheese combined.

3) On a floured work surface, flatten the dough ball with your fingertips and stretch it into a 12-inch (30 cm) round. (See page 13.)

4) Sprinkle a pizza peel with cornmeal and lay the pizza dough round on it. Spread the tomato sauce onto the pizza dough, leaving $\frac{1}{2}$ to $\frac{3}{4}$ inch (1.3 to 2 cm) of dough uncovered around the outside edge. Scatter the garlic and capers and sprinkle the oregano on top of the tomato sauce. Place the sliced zucchini and eggplant evenly around the pizza. Scatter the cheeses on top of the vegetables. Arrange the rings of red pepper and onion evenly on top of the cheese **(A)**. Sprinkle with salt and drizzle with olive oil.

5) Give the peel a quick shake to be sure the pizza is not sticking to the peel. Slide the pizza off the peel onto the stone in the oven. Broil for 1 minute. Turn the oven temperature to the highest bake setting and cook for 5 minutes. Quickly open the oven door, pull out the rack, and with a pair of tongs, rotate the pizza (not the stone) a half turn. Cook for 5 minutes more.

6) Using the peel, remove the pizza from the oven. Cut into slices and serve.

Greg's Beer Cooler: Belgian Saison

What the saison expresses in the glass, the Pizza Siciliana expresses on the plate. The variety of toppings on the pizza and the intricacy of flavors in the beer fully complement each other. Both exhibit a beautiful balance, elegant complexity, bright fruitiness, and dry earthiness.

Greg's Pick: Brasserie Dupont Saison Dupont Vieille Provision

---

MAKES ONE 12-INCH (30 CM) PIZZA

2 ounces (55 g) fresh cow's milk mozzarella

2 ounces (55 g) Pecorino Toscano cheese (see page 21)

1 ball Paradiso Pizza Dough (page 27)

Cornmeal, for sprinkling

¾ cup (170 g) Winter Tomato Sauce (page 28)

1 teaspoon chopped garlic

1 teaspoon capers

1 teaspoon chopped fresh oregano

10 very thin slices zucchini

7 very thin slices Italian eggplant

7 (¼-inch, or 6 mm) rings red bell pepper

5 very thin slices red onion

Kosher salt, to taste

Olive oil, for drizzling

PIZZA ATOMICA

With its blast of flavors from the crushed red pepper flakes, the hearty salami, and the briny olives, this pizza lives up to its name. We use Casalingo salami at Pizzeria Paradiso—aged but not dry, hearty and rustic in flavor, and coarse and fat in texture—to give that distinctive Atomica flavor. You may use any salami of your choice to develop a flavor that suits your taste, and use more or less crushed red pepper flakes according to your desired level of spiciness.

1) Place a pizza stone on the top rack of a cool oven. Set the oven to broil and preheat for 30 minutes.

2) Cut the mozzarella into ⅓-inch (about 1 cm) dice. You should have about ¾ cup (115 g).

3) On a floured work surface, flatten the dough ball with your fingertips and stretch it into a 12-inch (30 cm) round. (See page 13.)

4) Sprinkle a pizza peel with cornmeal and lay the pizza dough round on it. Spread the tomato sauce onto the pizza dough, leaving ½ to ¾ inch (1.3 to 2 cm) of dough uncovered around the outside edge. Place the slices of salami evenly around the pizza **(A)**. Place the olives on top of the salami and sauce. Sprinkle the pizza with the crushed red pepper flakes. Scatter the cheese evenly over the other toppings. Sprinkle with salt and drizzle with olive oil.

5) Give the peel a quick shake to be sure the pizza is not sticking to the peel. Slide the pizza off the peel onto the stone in the oven. Broil for 1 minute. Turn the oven temperature to the highest bake setting and cook for 5 minutes. Quickly open the oven door, pull out the rack, and with a pair of tongs, rotate the pizza (not the stone) a half turn. Cook for 5 minutes more.

6) Using the peel, remove the pizza from the oven. Cut into slices and serve.

A

MAKES ONE 12-INCH (30 CM) PIZZA

4 ounces (115 g) fresh cow's milk mozzarella

1 ball Paradiso Pizza Dough (page 27)

Cornmeal, for sprinkling

¾ cup (170 g) Winter Tomato Sauce (page 28)

1½ ounces (43 g) salami, thinly sliced

¼ cup (25 g) pitted, halved Kalamata olives (see page 23)

¼ teaspoon crushed red pepper flakes

Kosher salt, to taste

Olive oil, for drizzling

Greg's Beer Cooler: IPA

Hop-forward IPAs pack a one-two punch when paired with this pizza. The bitter alpha acids in the hops cut through the fatty country salami, while the hops' citrus notes intensify the saltiness of the olives. This pairing will knock you off your feet.

Greg's Pick: Three Floyds Zombie Dust

PIZZA GENOVESE

Once when visiting Rome, I tasted a regional favorite: white pizza topped with potatoes. Those of you raised on the notion that meals should never contain more than one starch might be able to imagine my excitement upon experiencing the thrill of two starches at once. When I opened Pizzeria Paradiso, I wanted to share that thrill with my customers. Thus the Genovese (named for Genoa, the birthplace of pesto) was born.

1) Place the potatoes in a 2-quart (2 L) pot. Cover with salted water and bring to a boil. Lower the heat to a simmer. Cook for 15 to 20 minutes or until the potatoes are tender. Remove from heat, drain, and cool. Slice the potatoes into ¼-inch-thick (6 mm) rounds.

2) Place a pizza stone on the top rack of a cool oven. Set the oven to broil and preheat for 30 minutes.

3) On a floured work surface, flatten the dough ball with your fingertips and stretch it into a 12-inch (30 cm) round. (See page 13.)

MAKES ONE
12-INCH (30 CM)
PIZZA

4 medium (about
2 inches, or 5 cm)
red potatoes

1 ball Paradiso Pizza
Dough (page 27)

Cornmeal, for
sprinkling

¼ cup (65 g) Basil Pesto

¼ cup plus 1 tablespoon
(30 g) freshly grated
Parmesan cheese

Kosher salt, to taste

Olive oil, for drizzling

4) Sprinkle a pizza peel with cornmeal and lay the pizza dough round on it. Spread the pesto onto the pizza dough, leaving ½ to ¾ inch (1.3 to 2 cm) of dough uncovered around the outside edge. Arrange the potato slices on top of the pesto. Sprinkle with ¼ cup (25 g) of the Parmesan cheese and salt. Drizzle liberally with oil.

5) Give the peel a quick shake to be sure the pizza is not sticking to the peel. Slide the pizza off the peel onto the stone in the oven. Broil for 1 minute. Turn the oven temperature to the highest bake setting and cook for 5 minutes. Quickly open the oven door, pull out the rack, and with a pair of tongs, rotate the pizza (not the stone) a half turn. Cook for 5 minutes more.

6) Using the peel, remove the pizza from the oven. Sprinkle with the remaining Parmesan cheese and drizzle with a little more olive oil. Cut into slices and serve.

Basil Pesto

1) Place the basil, pine nuts, and garlic cloves in the bowl of a food processor. Process until finely chopped.

2) Add the cheese and process until blended.

3) With the motor running, slowly add the olive oil.

4) Add the salt and a few grindings of pepper.

MAKES 1 CUP
(260 G)

3 cups (100 g)
loosely packed fresh
basil leaves

2 tablespoons (18 g)
pine nuts

1 ½ cloves garlic

¼ cup plus 2 tablespoons
(35 g) freshly grated
Parmesan cheese

2 tablespoons (28 ml)
olive oil

⅛ teaspoon kosher salt

Freshly ground black
pepper to taste

Greg's Beer Cooler: English-Style Brown Ale

A simple pizza with a straightforward potato sweetness melds with the subdued maltiness of a brown ale. The garlic and pine nuts of the pesto mirror the nuttiness of the ale. To borrow from Leonardo da Vinci, "Simplicity is the ultimate sophistication."

Greg's Pick: Samuel Smith's Nut Brown Ale

PIZZA BOTTARGA

Think of this pizza as eggs two ways. Number one is chicken eggs that bake in the oven right on top of the pizza. Number two is salt-cured fish roe, or *bottarga*, sprinkled over the cooked pie. Together, the two types of eggs merge land and sea, offering a new kind of "surf and turf." Locate *bottarga* at specialty or Italian food stores or online. The unusual ingredients and slightly involved cooking instructions may scare the novice pizzaiolo. But fear not; you'll be an old hand after the first try.

1) Place a pizza stone on the top rack of a cool oven. Set the oven to broil and preheat for 30 minutes.

2) On a floured work surface, flatten the dough ball with your fingertips and stretch it into a 12-inch (30 cm) round. (See page 13.)

3) Sprinkle a pizza peel with cornmeal and lay the pizza dough round on it. Spread the tomato sauce onto the pizza dough, leaving $1/2$ to $3/4$ inch (1.3 to 2 cm) of dough uncovered around the outside edge. Scatter the garlic and sprinkle the parsley on top of the tomato sauce. Sprinkle with $1/4$ cup (25 g) of the Parmesan cheese and the salt. Drizzle with oil.

4) Crack the eggs into a small bowl.

5) Give the peel a quick shake to be sure the pizza is not sticking to the peel. Slide the pizza off the peel onto the stone in the oven. Broil for 1 minute.

6) Open the oven door and pull out the rack. Holding the rack level if necessary, carefully pour the eggs onto the pizza, keeping the yolks intact **(A)**. Quickly slide the rack back into the oven and close the oven door. Turn the oven temperature to the highest bake setting and cook for 5 minutes.

7) Again, quickly open the oven door, pull out the rack, and with a pair of tongs, rotate the pizza (not the stone) a half turn. Cook for 2 to 3 minutes more or until the whites of the eggs are just set and the yolks are still runny.

8) Using the peel, remove the pizza from the oven. Sprinkle with the bottarga and the remaining Parmesan cheese. Drizzle with oil.

9) Transfer the pizza to a serving platter. Break the egg yolks with a fork and spread them evenly around the pizza. Cut into slices and serve.

A

MAKES ONE 12-INCH (30 CM) PIZZA

1 ball Paradiso Pizza Dough (page 27)

Cornmeal, for sprinkling

¾ cup (170 g) Winter Tomato Sauce (page 28)

1 teaspoon chopped garlic

1 tablespoon (4 g) chopped fresh Italian parsley

¼ cup plus 1 tablespoon (30 g) freshly grated Parmesan cheese

Kosher salt, to taste

Olive oil, for drizzling

3 large eggs

2 teaspoons grated bottarga

Greg's Beer Cooler: Belgian Dubbel

I like roasted malts with tomato. Here a Belgian *dubbel*, with its nutty, rich, malt-forward flavors, plays the part, while its high alcohol content acts like liquid bread, sopping up the runny egg yolks.

Greg's Pick: Westmalle Dubbel

SAUCES

Now comes the fun! After spending several chapters demonstrating the basics through a variety of doughs, tomato sauces, and methods, it's time to have fun. This chapter brings new meaning to "playing with your food" by pulling together ideas and combinations that may never have occurred to you.

While several of the sauces and flavors of the pizzas in this level originate in Italy, we venture outside the Italian borders for others. With Black Bean Sauce, we travel to Cuba. With Creamy Parmesan Sauce, we make a pizza that tastes like a bowl of clam chowder. And with homemade barbecue sauce, okra, corn, and pork, we drop in on a Southern American Sunday dinner.

This level contains seven pizzas, each with a different sauce or spread and garnished with complementary toppings. Thus Roasted Red Pepper Sauce is paired with eggplant and goat cheese, and Salsa Verde is teamed with artichokes and sausage. You will find both the simple and the more complex. With all of them you will find intricate flavors that will spur your creativity and encourage you to develop playful pizzas of your own.

ROASTED RED PEPPER SAUCE

Don't be afraid of the dark. This pizza's depth of flavor relies on your trusting yourself to burn the skins of the red peppers. As you do so, the pepper flesh will roast and take on a sweet, earthy flavor. With the meaty flavor of the eggplant and olives and the sweetness of the raisins, each bite of this pizza reveals the pleasure and complexity of the dark side.

1) Place a pizza stone on the top rack of a cool oven. Set the oven to broil and preheat for 30 minutes.

2) In a small bowl, cover the raisins with hot water, soak for 5 minutes, and then drain.

3) Heat the oil in a large sauté pan over medium heat. Add the onion and cook until soft, 5 to 10 minutes. Turn the heat to medium-high and then add the eggplant and brown. Stir in the raisin, olives, and pine nuts and cook for 3 minutes more (A). Remove from the heat and cool.

4) Crumble the goat cheese into 1/3-inch (about 1 cm) pieces. You should have about 3/4 cup (115 g).

5) On a floured work surface, flatten the dough ball with your fingertips and stretch it into a 12-inch (30 cm) round. (See page 13.)

6) Sprinkle a pizza peel with cornmeal and lay the pizza dough round on it. Spread the Roasted Red Pepper Sauce on top of the pizza dough, leaving 1/2 to 3/4 inch (1.3 to 2 cm) of dough uncovered around the outside edge. Scatter the eggplant mixture on top of the sauce. Lay the spinach leaves evenly over the eggplant. Scatter the goat cheese over the spinach. Sprinkle the pizza with salt and drizzle with oil.

7) Give the peel a quick shake to be sure the pizza is not sticking to the peel. Slide the pizza off the peel onto the stone in the oven. Broil for 1 minute. Turn the oven temperature to the highest bake setting and cook for 5 minutes. Quickly open the oven door, pull out the rack, and with a pair of tongs, rotate the pizza (not the stone) a half turn. Cook for 5 minutes more.

8) Using the peel, remove the pizza from the oven. Cut into slices and serve.

A

MAKES ONE 12-INCH (30 CM) PIZZA

1/4 cup (35 g) raisins

3 tablespoons (45 ml) olive oil, plus more for drizzling

1 small onion, diced

2 cups (164 g) diced eggplant

1/4 cup (25 g) chopped, pitted Ligurian olives (see page 23)

2 tablespoons (18 g) pine nuts

4 ounces (115 g) fresh goat cheese

1 ball Paradiso, New York–Style, or Whole Wheat Pizza Dough (page 27, 31, or 42)

Cornmeal, for sprinkling

3/4 cup (170 g) Roasted Red Pepper Sauce (page 88)

1 1/2 cups (45 g) loosely packed spinach leaves

Kosher salt, to taste

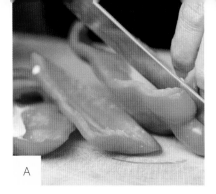

A

B

C

Roasted Red Pepper Sauce

MAKES 1 ¼ CUPS
(280 G)

4 whole red bell peppers

1 tablespoon (15 ml) olive oil

1 cup (160 g) chopped onion

1 teaspoon finely chopped garlic

½ teaspoon chopped fresh oregano

1 teaspoon chopped fresh thyme

1 teaspoon red wine vinegar

½ teaspoon kosher salt

Freshly ground black pepper to taste

1) Set the oven to broil.

2) Cut the red pepper flesh from the stem, core, and seeds by making 4 cuts lengthwise **(A)**. The result will be 4 large flat pieces per pepper.

3) Place the pepper pieces skin side up on a baking sheet lined with aluminum foil or a silicone baking liner. Slide the pan under the broiler and cook until the peppers' skin is charred all over **(B)**. Remove the peppers from the oven and transfer to a medium bowl. Cover the bowl with plastic wrap and let cool.

4) When the peppers have cooled, peel them. In peeling the peppers, you will find that where the skin is completely charred, it easily slips from the pepper.

5) Place the peppers in the bowl of a food processor and process until smooth.

6) In a medium pot, heat the oil over medium heat until warm. Add the onions and cook 5 to 10 minutes or until soft.

7) Turn the heat to low and add the garlic, oregano, and thyme. Cook for another minute or two until fragrant, stirring often to ensure the garlic does not burn.

8) Stir in the red pepper puree, the vinegar, salt, and a few grindings of pepper. Increase the heat to medium and bring to a boil. Lower the heat and simmer for about 30 minutes to develop the flavor **(C)**. Remove from the heat and cool.

9) Store in the refrigerator for up to 3 days or freeze for longer storage.

BLACK BEAN SAUCE

The pickled onions bring a bright flavor to this hearty Latin American-inspired pie, making it a colorful feast for both your eyes and your taste buds. Increase the jalapeño in the sauce or add some chopped chile peppers to the pizza for a spicier touch.

1) Place a pizza stone on the top rack of a cool oven. Set the oven to broil and preheat for 30 minutes.

2) Cut the cheese into ⅓-inch (about 1 cm) dice.

3) Toss the onions with the vinegar and a pinch of salt and sugar. Let stand for at least 5 to 10 minutes to pickle the onions.

4) On a floured work surface, flatten the dough ball with your fingertips and stretch it into a 12-inch (30 cm) round. (See page 13.)

5) Sprinkle a pizza peel with cornmeal and lay the pizza dough round on it. Spread the Black Bean Sauce onto the pizza dough, leaving ½ to ¾ inch (1.3 to 2 cm) of dough uncovered around the outside edge. Scatter the cherry tomatoes, corn, and red pepper evenly over the sauce. Sprinkle with 1 tablespoon (1 g) of the cilantro. Scatter the cheese on top of the pizza. Sprinkle the pizza with salt and drizzle with olive oil **(A)**.

6) Give the peel a quick shake to be sure the pizza is not sticking to the peel. Slide the pizza off the peel onto the stone in the oven. Broil for 1 minute. Turn the oven temperature to the highest bake setting and cook for 5 minutes. Quickly open the oven door, pull out the rack, and with a pair of tongs, rotate the pizza (not the stone) a half turn. Cook for 5 minutes more.

7) Meanwhile, remove the pit from the avocado, peel it, and cut into 12 to 15 thin slices.

8) Using the peel, remove the pizza from the oven.

9) Arrange the avocado slices on top of the pizza and dot with the sour cream. Drain the onions and lay them evenly over the avocado and sour cream. Scatter the remaining cilantro leaves over the pizza. Cut into slices and serve.

A

MAKES ONE 12-INCH (30 CM) PIZZA

4 ounces (115 g) pepper Jack cheese

5 very thin slices red onion

1 teaspoon red wine vinegar

Kosher salt, to taste

Pinch of sugar

1 ball Whole Wheat, Multigrain, or Paradiso Pizza Dough (page 42, 46, or 27)

Cornmeal, for sprinkling

¾ cup (170 g) Black Bean Sauce

½ cup (75 g) halved cherry tomatoes

½ cup (77 g) corn kernels

¼ cup (38 g) chopped red bell pepper

3 tablespoons (3 g) chopped fresh cilantro

Olive oil, for drizzling

½ avocado

3 tablespoons (45 g) sour cream

B

Black Bean Sauce

1) Heat the oil in a sauté pan over medium heat until warm. Add the onion, celery, and carrot and cook for 10 minutes or until the vegetables are soft.

2) Turn the heat to low. Add the jalapeño, garlic, coriander, and cumin and cook for a minute or two until fragrant, stirring often to ensure the garlic does not burn.

3) Add the black beans and crushed tomato. Add salt and pepper and continue cooking until the liquid has thickened to a saucy consistency, about 10 to 15 minutes. Remove from heat and let cool **(B)**.

4) Place half of the sauce in the bowl of a food processor and puree until smooth. Return the pureed mixture to the pot with the unpureed sauce. Mix well.

5) Store in the refrigerator for up to 3 days.

MAKES ABOUT 2 CUPS
(455 G)

1 tablespoon (15 ml) olive oil

½ cup (80 g) chopped onion

¼ cup (25 g) chopped celery

¼ cup (33 g) chopped carrot

1½ teaspoons finely chopped jalapeño pepper

¼ teaspoon chopped garlic

Pinch of ground coriander

Pinch of ground cumin

¾ cup (129 g) cooked black beans

¾ cup (135 g) canned crushed tomato

Kosher salt, to taste

Freshly ground black pepper to taste

CREAMY PARMESAN SAUCE

The pizzaiolo goes to New England for this clam chowder–inspired pizza, complete with bacon, potatoes, and thyme. I instruct you to place live clams in their shells on top of this pizza. The clams cook as the pizza cooks, releasing their briny flavor directly onto the pizza and causing it to be a tad wet in the center. You will need to extract the clams and remove the shells before eating the pie. Messy? Yes, but worth it.

1) Place a pizza stone on the top rack of a cool oven. Set the oven to broil and preheat for 30 minutes.

2) Place the potatoes in a small pot and cover with water. Add salt until the water tastes like salted water. Bring the water to a boil over high heat. Simmer for 5 minutes and then drain. The potatoes should be cooked but still retain their shape.

3) In a sauté pan, cook the bacon until it begins to brown and loses some of its fat. Remove the bacon pieces from the pan and drain on paper towels.

4) Scrub the shells of the clams.

5) On a floured work surface, flatten the dough ball with your fingertips and stretch it into a 12-inch (30 cm) round. (See page 13.)

6) Sprinkle a pizza peel with cornmeal and lay the pizza dough round on it. Spread the Creamy Parmesan sauce onto the pizza dough, leaving 1/2 to 3/4 inch (1.3 to 2 cm) of dough uncovered around the outside edge. Scatter the potatoes and bacon over the sauce. Sprinkle the pizza with the parsley, thyme, and 2 tablespoons (10 g) of the Parmesan cheese. Place the clams evenly around the pizza. Arrange the rings of onion evenly on top of the clams **(A)**. Drizzle with olive oil.

7) Give the peel a quick shake to be sure the pizza is not sticking to the peel. Slide the pizza off the peel onto the stone in the oven. Broil for 1 minute. Turn the oven temperature to the highest bake setting and cook for 5 minutes. Quickly open the oven door, pull out the rack, and with a pair of tongs, rotate the pizza (not the stone) a half turn. Cook for 5 minutes more.

8) Using the peel, remove the pizza from the oven. Sprinkle with the remaining Parmesan cheese. Let the pizza stand for a minute or two to absorb the clam liquor. Cut into slices and serve.

A

MAKES ONE 12-INCH (30 CM) PIZZA

3/4 cup (83 g) diced russet potatoes (1/2-inch, or 1.3 cm, dice)

Kosher salt, to taste

2 ounces (55 g) thickly sliced bacon, cut into 1/2-inch (1.3 cm) pieces

10 to 12 small littleneck clams in their shells

1 ball Paradiso Pizza Dough (page 27)

Cornmeal, for sprinkling

2/3 cup (160 ml) Creamy Parmesan Sauce (page 94)

1 tablespoon (4 g) chopped fresh Italian parsley

1/2 teaspoon finely chopped fresh thyme

3 tablespoons (15 g) Parmesan cheese

5 very thin slices red onion

Olive oil, for drizzling

Creamy Parmesan Sauce

1) In a small pot, melt the butter over medium heat. Add the onion and celery and cook for 5 to 10 minutes or until soft. Turn the heat to low.

2) Meanwhile, in a separate small pot, scald (heat to just below the boiling point) the clam juice and heavy cream over medium heat.

3) Add the flour to the butter and vegetables. Continue to cook for several minutes, stirring often. The flour may turn golden, but do not let it brown.

4) Using a whisk, slowly add the warm liquid to the onion mixture. Continue whisking until smooth (**A**).

5) Cook over low heat for 20 minutes, making sure that the sauce does not boil. Remove from the heat and stir in the Parmesan cheese. Season lightly with salt and pepper.

2 tablespoons (28 g) butter

2 tablespoons (20 g) finely chopped onion

2 tablespoons (13 g) finely chopped celery

½ cup (120 ml) clam juice

½ cup (120 ml) heavy cream

1½ tablespoons (12 g) all-purpose flour

2 tablespoons (10 g) freshly grated Parmesan cheese

Kosher salt, to taste

Freshly ground pepper to taste

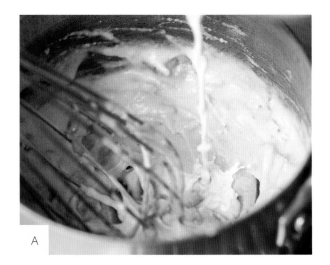

A

ELEPHANT GARLIC PESTO

A relative of both onion and garlic, elephant garlic marries the two flavors, producing a sweet, milder garlic taste. If you prefer a more pungent garlic flavor, throw a large clove of raw garlic in with the elephant garlic when you process it. You can use this pesto as an alternative to fresh garlic on many of the pizzas in this book.

1) Place a pizza stone on the top rack of a cool oven. Preheat the oven to 450°F (230°C, or gas mark 8).

2) Cut the red pepper into 1-inch (2.5 cm) pieces. Toss with the oil and sprinkle with salt. Scatter the peppers in a single layer on a baking sheet lined with aluminum foil or a silicone baking liner. Place on the middle rack of the oven and roast for 15 to 20 minutes. Remove the peppers from the oven and let cool.

3) Turn the oven to broil and preheat for 30 minutes.

4) On a floured work surface, flatten the dough ball with your fingertips and stretch it into a 12-inch (30 cm) round. (See page 13.)

5) Sprinkle a pizza peel with cornmeal and lay the pizza dough round on it. Spread the Elephant Garlic Pesto onto the pizza dough, leaving $1/2$ to $3/4$ inch (1.3 to 2 cm) of dough uncovered around the outside edge. Lay the spinach leaves on top of the pesto. Sprinkle with the pine nuts and parsley. Scatter the roasted pepper pieces and cheese on top of the pesto and spinach (A). Arrange the onion rings evenly on top of the cheese. Sprinkle the pizza with salt and drizzle with olive oil.

6) Give the peel a quick shake to be sure the pizza is not sticking to the peel. Slide the pizza off the peel onto the stone in the oven. Broil for 1 minute. Turn the oven temperature to the highest bake setting and cook for 5 minutes. Quickly open the oven door, pull out the rack, and with a pair of tongs, rotate the pizza (not the stone) a half turn. Cook for 5 minutes more.

7) Using the peel, remove the pizza from the oven. Cut into slices and serve.

MAKES ONE 12-INCH (30 CM) PIZZA

1 red bell pepper

1½ teaspoons olive oil, plus more for drizzling

Kosher salt to taste

1 ball Paradiso Pizza Dough (page 27)

Cornmeal, for sprinkling

½ cup (115 g) Elephant Garlic Pesto

2 cups (60 g) loosely packed baby spinach leaves

2 tablespoons (18 g) pine nuts

1 tablespoon (4 g) chopped fresh Italian parsley

3 ounces (85 g) fresh buffalo mozzarella, torn into 10 to 12 pieces

5 very thin slices red onion

Elephant Garlic Pesto

1) Preheat the oven to 400°F (200°C, or gas mark 6).

2) Break the head of garlic apart and peel each clove. Rub a square of aluminum foil big enough to enclose the whole cloves of garlic with 1 tablespoon (15 ml) oil. Wrap the garlic in the foil and crimp closed. Place the wrapped garlic in a baking pan and put it in the oven. Bake for 30 to 45 minutes until the garlic is very soft. Remove the garlic from the oven, remove the foil, and cool **(A)**.

3) Place the garlic and pine nuts in the bowl of a food processor. Process until finely chopped.

4) Add the Parmesan cheese and process until blended.

5) With the motor running, slowly add the remaining olive oil.

6) Add the salt and a few grindings of pepper **(B)**.

MAKES 1 CUP (225 G)

1 head elephant garlic

¼ cup (60 ml) olive oil

¼ cup (35 g) pine nuts

¼ cup (25 g) freshly grated Parmesan cheese

¼ teaspoon kosher salt

Freshly ground black pepper to taste

A

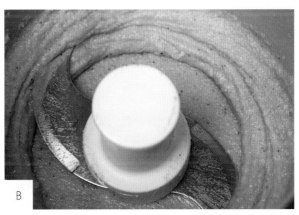

B

SALSA VERDE

Salsa Verde, an Italian condiment generally used as a dipping sauce for meat and fish, plays a robust role on this pizza. It serves as the foundation complementing the vegetables and sausage that top it. Serve the extra sauce on the side for those who want a bigger burst of flavor.

1) Place a pizza stone on the top rack of a cool oven. Set the oven to broil and preheat for 30 minutes.

2) Heat the oil in a large sauté pan over medium heat. Add the onion and sauté for 5 to 10 minutes or until soft. Add the radicchio and continue cooking for several minutes or until the radicchio has wilted **(A)**. Season to taste with salt and pepper. Remove from the heat and let cool.

3) Cut the cheese into 1/3-inch (about 1 cm) dice. You should have about 2/3 cup (115 g).

4) On a floured work surface, flatten the dough ball with your fingertips and stretch it into a 12-inch (30 cm) round. (See page 13.)

5) Sprinkle a pizza peel with cornmeal and lay the pizza dough round on it. Spread the Salsa Verde onto the pizza dough, leaving 1/2 to 3/4 inch (1.3 to 2 cm) of dough uncovered around the outside edge. Scatter the radicchio and onion mixture on top of the pesto. Arrange the artichokes evenly around the pizza. Scatter the cheese on top of the vegetables. Evenly dot the pizza with small pieces of the sausage. Sprinkle the pizza with salt and drizzle with olive oil.

6) Give the peel a quick shake to be sure the pizza is not sticking to the peel. Slide the pizza off the peel onto the stone in the oven. Broil for 1 minute. Turn the oven temperature to the highest bake setting and cook for 5 minutes. Quickly open the oven door, pull out the rack, and with a pair of tongs, rotate the pizza (not the stone) a half turn. Cook for 5 minutes more.

7) Using the peel, remove the pizza from the oven. Cut into slices and serve.

> ### MAKES ONE 12-INCH (30 CM) PIZZA
>
> 2 tablespoons (28 ml) olive oil, plus more for drizzling
>
> 1/2 medium onion, sliced
>
> 1/2 head small radicchio, cored and sliced
>
> Kosher salt, to taste
>
> Freshly ground black pepper, to taste
>
> 4 ounces (115 g) Pecorino Toscano cheese (see page 21)
>
> 1 ball Paradiso Pizza Dough (page 27)
>
> Cornmeal, for sprinkling
>
> 1/3 cup (87 g) Salsa Verde (page 100)
>
> 16 artichoke quarters
>
> 2 1/2 ounces (70 g) bulk pork sausage (see page 22)

Greg's Beer Cooler: American Saison

A heavily hopped American saison pairs bitter hops with bitter radicchio and bright pilsner malt with the bright herbs and lemon of the pesto. It's simple yet complex.

Greg's Pick: Oxbow Farmhouse Pale Ale

A

A

B

Salsa Verde

1) Place the parsley, garlic, capers, anchovies, lemon zest and juice, and red pepper flakes in the bowl of a food processor (**A**). Process until finely chopped (**B**).

2) With the motor running, slowly add the olive oil.

3) Add the salt and a few grindings of pepper.

MAKES ¾ CUP (195 G)

3½ cups (210 g) loosely packed fresh Italian parsley

2 cloves garlic

2 tablespoons (17 g) capers

1 tablespoon (15 g) chopped anchovy fillets (about 4 fillets)

Zest of 2 lemons

Juice of 1½ lemons

Pinch of crushed red pepper flakes

2 tablespoons (28 ml) olive oil

¼ teaspoon kosher salt

Freshly ground black pepper, to taste

BARBECUE SAUCE

A Southern feast greets you with every bite of this pizza. Roasting the okra until it's nicely browned will eliminate the viscous quality that you sometimes find in okra dishes. You can use leftover pork, or cook pork just for this. To give the pizza a bigger burst of flavor, barbecue a pork butt and use the barbecue sauce to baste it (or braise the pork butt in the sauce). Then use the pork to top the pizza.

1) Place a pizza stone on the top rack of a cool oven. Preheat the oven to 450°F (230°C, or gas mark 8).

2) Cut the okra in half lengthwise. Place the okra in a small bowl and toss with 1 teaspoon of the oil, a pinch of salt, and a grinding of pepper.

3) Turn the okra into a large roasting pan lined with aluminum foil or a silicone baking liner. Lay each piece cut side down in a single layer. Roast for 15 to 25 minutes until they are soft and some pieces show significant browning **(A)**. Remove the okra from the oven and cool.

4) Set the oven to broil and preheat for 30 minutes.

5) Cut the cheese into $1/3$-inch (about 1 cm) dice. You should have about $3/4$ cup (115 g).

6) Cut the pork into $1/2$-inch (1.3 cm) dice or tear into 1-inch (2.5 cm) pieces. You should have about $3/4$ cup (115 g).

7) Cut the tomato into a $1/4$-inch (6 mm) dice. You should have about $1/4$ cup (45 g).

8) On a generously floured work surface, flatten the dough ball with your fingertips and stretch it into a 12-inch (30 cm) round. (See page 13.)

9) Sprinkle a pizza peel with cornmeal and lay the pizza dough round on it. Spread the Barbecue Sauce onto the pizza dough, leaving $1/2$ to $3/4$ inch (1.3 to 2 cm) of dough uncovered around the outside edge. Scatter the pork, okra, corn, tomatoes, and cheese evenly over the sauce. Arrange the onion rings over the cheese. Sprinkle the pizza with salt and drizzle with oil.

10) Give the peel a quick shake to be sure the pizza is not sticking to the peel. Slide the pizza off the peel onto the stone in the oven. Broil for 1 minute. Turn the oven temperature to the highest bake setting and cook for 5 minutes. Quickly open the oven door, pull out the rack, and with a pair of tongs rotate the pizza (not the stone) a half turn. Cook for 5 minutes more.

11) Using the peel, remove the pizza from the oven. Cut into slices and serve.

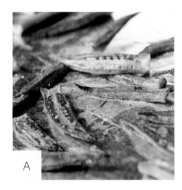

A

MAKES ONE 12-INCH (30 CM) PIZZA

8 medium okra

1 teaspoon olive oil, plus more for drizzling

Kosher salt, to taste

Freshly ground black pepper, to taste

4 ounces (115 g) cheddar cheese

4 ounces (115 g) cooked pork

½ small green tomato

1 ball Multigrain, Whole Wheat, or Paradiso Pizza Dough (page 46, 42, or 27)

Cornmeal, for sprinkling

¾ cup (188 g) Barbecue Sauce

¼ cup (39 g) fresh or frozen corn kernels

5 very thin slices red onion

Barbecue Sauce

A

1) In a medium pot, heat the oil over medium heat until warm. Add the onion cook for 5 to 10 minutes or until soft.

2) Turn the heat to low and add the garlic, thyme, red pepper flakes, ground mustard, paprika, salt, pepper, allspice, and cloves. Cook for another minute or two until fragrant, stirring often to ensure the garlic and spices do not burn.

3) Stir in the remaining ingredients, increase the heat to medium, and bring to a boil. Lower the heat and simmer for about 1 hour to develop the flavor **(A)**. Remove from the heat and cool.

4) Store the sauce in the refrigerator for up to 3 days or freeze for longer storage.

Greg's Beer Cooler: Weizen Doppelbock

This pairing of an elegant German beer and a heavy-handed American country pizza looks, on paper, like it shouldn't work. However, the natural by-product of fermenting with hefeweizen yeast is an unmistakable clove flavor that complements the spices in the barbecue sauce, while the subtle sweetness of the dark malts play with the natural sweetness of summer corn. Sometimes your taste buds know better than your logical mind.

Greg's Pick: Schneider & Sohn Aventinus

MAKES ABOUT 2 ½ CUPS (625 G)

1 tablespoon (15 ml) olive oil

1 cup (160 g) diced onion

1 tablespoon (10 g) chopped garlic

½ teaspoon finely chopped fresh thyme

½ teaspoon crushed red pepper flakes

½ teaspoon ground mustard

¼ teaspoon paprika

1 teaspoon salt

¼ teaspoon freshly ground black pepper

Pinch of ground allspice

Pinch of ground cloves

2 cups (360 g) canned crushed tomatoes

¼ cup (60 ml) stout beer

2½ tablespoons (36 ml) apple cider vinegar

2 tablespoons (28 ml) freshly squeezed orange juice

4 teaspoons (20 ml) Worcestershire sauce

4 teaspoons (27 g) molasses

½ teaspoon freshly squeezed lemon juice

⅛ teaspoon Tabasco sauce

1 small bay leaf

RICOTTA CHEESE SPREAD

Start with a good-quality, creamy ricotta—the fresher, the better. Follow the full recipe below or use the ricotta spread as the base for numerous variations on white pizzas or calzones.

1) Place a pizza stone on the top rack of a cool oven. Preheat the oven to 400°F (200°C, or gas mark 6).

2) Remove the stems from the mushrooms and discard. Cut into 1-inch (2.5 cm) pieces. Peel and thickly slice the onion.

3) Place the mushrooms and onions in a large bowl. Add 2 tablespoons (28 ml) of the olive oil, ¼ teaspoon of the salt, and a few grindings of pepper. Toss the onions and mushrooms until they are evenly coated with the oil, salt, and pepper.

4) Turn the mushrooms and onions into two large roasting pans lined with aluminum foil or a silicone baking liner. Scatter the vegetables in a single layer in the pans. Roast for 15 to 20 minutes until the vegetables are soft and some pieces show significant browning **(A)**. Remove the vegetables from the oven and cool.

5) Set the oven to broil and preheat for 30 minutes. Heat 1 tablespoon (15 ml) of the olive oil in a small sauté pan over low heat until warm. Add the garlic and cook for a minute or two until fragrant, stirring often to ensure the garlic does not burn. Remove from the heat.

6) Place the ricotta cheese in a small bowl. Add the cooked garlic, ¼ teaspoon salt, and a few grindings of pepper. Mix well.

7) On a floured work surface, flatten the dough ball with your fingertips and stretch it into a 12-inch (30 cm) round. (See page 13.)

8) Sprinkle a pizza peel with cornmeal and lay the pizza dough round on it. Spread half of the ricotta cheese mixture onto the pizza dough, leaving ½ to ¾ inch (1.3 to 2 cm) of dough uncovered around the outside edge. Sprinkle with the pine nuts and thyme. Scatter 1¼ cups (280 g) of the roasted onions and mushrooms on top of the cheese. Dot the pizza with the remaining ricotta. Sprinkle the pizza with salt and drizzle with olive oil.

9) Give the peel a quick shake to be sure the pizza is not sticking to the peel. Slide the pizza off the peel onto the stone in the oven. Broil for 1 minute. Turn the oven temperature to the highest bake setting and cook for 5 minutes. Quickly open the oven door, pull out the rack, and with a pair of tongs, rotate the pizza (not the stone) a half turn. Cook for 5 minutes more.

10) Using the peel, remove the pizza from the oven. Drizzle with truffle oil. Cut into slices and serve.

A

MAKES ONE 12-INCH (30 CM) PIZZA

10 ounces (280 g) mixed wild mushrooms

1 large onion

3 tablespoons (45 ml) olive oil, plus more for drizzling

½ teaspoon kosher salt, plus more to taste

Freshly ground black pepper to taste

1 teaspoon chopped garlic

1 cup (250 g) ricotta cheese

1 ball Paradiso Pizza Dough (page 27)

Cornmeal, for sprinkling

2 tablespoons (18 g) pine nuts

½ teaspoon finely chopped fresh thyme

Truffle oil, for drizzling (optional)

PROTEINS

We all know the mainstay protein pizza topping: not simply cheese, but mozzarella cheese. But should we stop there? Can we use other proteins with cheese? Or can we imagine pizza with other proteins instead of cheese?

In this level, we throw the protein cupboard wide open. We explore fish and fowl. We use eggs and beans. While some proteins must cook in two phases—before and during the pizza's cooking—others cook just once, as the pizza itself cooks.

The proteins chosen for this level represent vast possibilities. I use chicken as an example of how you can use a wide variety of meats. I have included seafood recipes with both shellfish and finfish for you to use as a base to build your own repertoire from the oceans and lakes of the world. Finally, we have chickpeas and tofu because beans offer a wonderful alternative source of protein not often considered as suitable for pizza.

This chapter invites you to explore new pizza territory by placing the signposts along the trail to tasty creations.

CHICKEN

When making chicken pizzas, I generally cook the chicken twice. In this recipe, I bake the chicken before using it to top the pizza. You can follow my lead and bake your chicken or choose another cooking method such as broiling, grilling, or roasting. The second cooking occurs when the pizza bakes. I use thighs because their high fat content helps keep the chicken moist through the double cooking. This pizza, based on Buffalo wings, needs a substantial dough to carry the robust flavors. I suggest using the Multigrain, Whole Wheat, or Paradiso.

1) Place a pizza stone on the top rack of a cool oven. Preheat the oven to 375°F (190°C, or gas mark 5).

2) Season the chicken with salt and pepper. Place the pieces in an oiled baking pan and bake for about 35 minutes or until tender when pierced with a fork. Remove the chicken from the oven and cool. Tear or cut the chicken into 1-inch (2.5 cm) pieces **(A)**. Set aside.

3) Set the oven to broil and preheat the pizza stone for 30 minutes.

4) Cut the cheese into 1/3-inch (about 1 cm) dice. You should have about 3/4 cup (115 g).

5) On a generously floured work surface, flatten the dough ball with your fingertips and stretch it into a 12-inch (30 cm) round. (See page 13.)

6) Sprinkle a pizza peel with cornmeal and lay the pizza dough round on it. Spread the Buffalo Sauce onto the pizza dough, leaving 1/2 to 3/4 inch (1.3 to 2 cm) of dough uncovered around the outside edge. Scatter the chicken and cheese evenly over the pizza. Arrange the rings of onion over the cheese. Sprinkle with salt and drizzle with oil.

7) Give the peel a quick shake to be sure the pizza is not sticking to the peel. Slide the pizza off the peel onto the stone in the oven. Broil for 1 minute. Turn the oven temperature to the highest bake setting and cook for 5 minutes. Quickly open the oven door, pull out the rack, and with a pair of tongs rotate the pizza (not the stone) a half turn. Cook for 5 minutes more.

8) Using the peel, remove the pizza from the oven. Cut into slices. Scatter the parsley, carrot, and celery over the pizza. Dot the Blue Cheese Dipping Sauce on top of the vegetables and serve.

A

MAKES ONE 12-INCH (30 CM) PIZZA

8 ounces (225 g) boneless, skinless chicken thighs

Kosher salt, to taste

Freshly ground black pepper to taste

Olive oil

4 ounces (115 g) Fontina cheese

1 ball Multigrain, Whole Wheat, or Paradiso Pizza Dough (page 46, 42, or 27)

Cornmeal, for sprinkling

1/2 cup (120 ml) Buffalo Sauce (page 110)

5 very thin slices red onion

1 tablespoon (4 g) chopped fresh Italian parsley

1/2 cup (65 g) julienned carrot

3/4 cup (75 g) julienned celery

1/2 cup (115 g) Blue Cheese Dipping Sauce (page 110)

Buffalo Sauce

1) Melt the butter in a medium sauté pan over medium heat. Add the onions and bell pepper and cook for 5 to 10 minutes or until soft.

2) Turn the heat to low and add the garlic, tomato, and habanero peppers. Cook for another minute or two until fragrant, stirring often to ensure the garlic does not burn.

3) Add the remaining ingredients. Increase the heat to medium and bring to a boil. Lower the heat and simmer for about 1 hour to develop the flavor. Remove from the heat and cool. Remove the whole peppers and discard.

4) Store the sauce in the refrigerator for up to 3 days or freeze for longer storage.

½ cup (112 g) butter

⅓ cup (55 g) diced onion

1 red bell pepper, diced

1 clove garlic, minced

⅓ cup (60 g) chopped fresh tomato

1 or 2 habanero peppers (see Note)

1 bottle (6-ounces, or 175 ml) Louisiana-style hot sauce

½ cup (120 ml) water

½ cup (120 ml) white vinegar

Juice of ½ lemon

¼ cup (60 g) ketchup

¾ teaspoon salt

Note: Habanero peppers, one of the hottest chile peppers available, give this sauce a distinct flavor. Using them whole allows them to flavor the sauce without adding excessive heat. If you want more heat, chop the peppers before adding them to the sauce. Proceed with caution according to your heat tolerance and wash your hands well with soap and water after handling these fiery peppers.

Blue Cheese Dipping Sauce

1) Heat the oil in a small sauté pan over medium heat until warm. Add the garlic pieces and cook for several minutes until the garlic is golden and fragrant but not burned. Scrape the oil and garlic pieces into a small bowl and cool.

2) Add the mayonnaise, cream, lemon juice, and parsley and stir until combined.

3) Fold in the blue cheese. Season with salt and pepper. Refrigerate for 2 to 4 hours. Remove the garlic pieces and discard.

4) Store in the refrigerator for up to 3 days.

1 tablespoon (15 ml) olive oil

2 cloves garlic, cut in half

¼ cup (60 g) mayonnaise

2 tablespoons (28 ml) heavy cream

1½ teaspoons freshly squeezed lemon juice

1½ teaspoons minced fresh Italian parsley

2 ounces (55 g) blue cheese, crumbled

Kosher salt, to taste

Freshly ground black pepper, to taste

EGGS

I love the versatility of eggs: coddled, scrambled, or hard cooked, not to mention the sauces, soufflés, and cakes that only they can create. I prepare and consume them in all their incarnations. This recipe uses hard-cooked eggs. Hard cooking older eggs will make peeling the eggs easier. Interested in other egg recipes? Pizza Bottarga on page 82 and the Banana Pizza on page 154 contain eggs prepared using different techniques.

1) Place a pizza stone on the top rack of a cool oven and set the oven to broil.

2) Place the eggs in a small pot and cover with water. Bring to a boil over high heat. Reduce the heat to medium-low and continue to cook for 5 minutes.

3) Remove the pot from the heat and drain. Cover the eggs with ice water. Crack the shell of each egg and submerge in the water for several minutes to loosen the shell. Peel the eggs using the tip of a spoon while keeping the egg moistened with the ice water **(A)**. Refrigerate the eggs; when chilled, slice into ¼-inch (6 mm) rounds.

4) In another small pot, place the oil, butter, 1 tablespoon (4 g) of the parsley, the garlic, and anchovies. Bring the mixture to a simmer over medium heat. Continue simmering for 3 to 4 minutes. Remove from the heat.

5) Cut the bell peppers into ½-inch (1.3 cm) slices. You should have about 1 cup. Cut the cheese into ⅓-inch (about 1 cm) dice. You should have about ½ cup (85 g).

6) On a floured work surface, flatten the dough ball with your fingertips and stretch it into a 12-inch (30 cm) round. (See page 13.)

7) Sprinkle a pizza peel with cornmeal and lay the pizza dough round on it. Scatter the caramelized onions around the dough, leaving ½ to ¾ inch (1.3 to 2 cm) of dough uncovered around the outside edge. Arrange the egg slices evenly over the onions. Sprinkle with the remaining parsley. Scatter the peppers and cheese over the onions and eggs. Sprinkle with salt. Spoon half of the anchovy mixture evenly over the pizza.

8) Give the peel a quick shake to be sure the pizza is not sticking. Slide the pizza off the peel onto the stone in the oven. Broil for 1 minute. Turn the oven temperature to the highest bake setting and cook for 5 minutes. Quickly open the oven door, pull out the rack, and with a pair of tongs, rotate the pizza (not the stone) a half turn. Cook for 5 to 6 minutes more. Using the peel, remove the pizza from the oven.

9) Spoon the remaining anchovy mixture around the pizza. Cut into slices and serve.

Greg's Beer Cooler: Vienna (Amber) Lager

The slightly sweet malt flavors of Vienna lagers match the sweetness in the roasted peppers to a tee. Plus, the beer's quaffability (and 6.2 ABV) allows you to unreservedly wash down the salt of the briny anchovies.

Greg's Pick: Great Lakes Brewing Company Eliot Ness

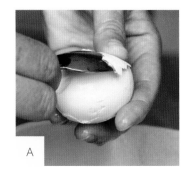

A

MAKES ONE 12-INCH (30 CM) PIZZA

3 large eggs

2 tablespoons (45 ml) olive oil

1 tablespoon (14 g) butter

2 tablespoons (8 g) chopped fresh Italian parsley

1 teaspoon chopped garlic

2 teaspoons finely chopped anchovy fillets

½ each roasted yellow and red bell peppers (see page 88)

3 ounces (85 g) Fontina cheese

1 ball Paradiso or Neapolitan–Style Pizza Dough (page 27 or 35)

Cornmeal, for sprinkling

¾ cup (115 g) caramelized onions (see page 61)

Kosher salt, to taste

SHRIMP

At Pizzeria Paradiso, we use fresh head-on shrimp to top our shrimp pizzas. You can use fresh or frozen shrimp or substitute other fish or shellfish. Just pay attention to the size of the fish pieces because you want them to cook thoroughly but not overcook and become dry.

1) Place a pizza stone on the top rack of a cool oven. Set the oven to broil and preheat for 30 minutes.

2) Peel and devein the shrimp. Cut each shrimp in half lengthwise (**A**). Set aside.

3) Peel the shallots and cut in half from root to tip. Laying each half flat on a cutting board, cut the shallots into thin slices. Set aside.

4) On a floured work surface, flatten the dough ball with your fingertips and stretch it into a 12-inch (30 cm) round. (See page 13.)

5) Sprinkle a pizza peel with cornmeal and lay the pizza dough round on it. Lay the arugula leaves on top of the pizza dough, leaving $1/2$ to $3/4$ inch (1.3 to 2 cm) of dough uncovered around the outside edge. Lay the shrimp evenly over the arugula (**B**). Sprinkle the lemon zest, dill, and $1/4$ cup (25 g) of the Parmesan cheese over the pizza. Scatter the shallot slices over the cheese. Sprinkle the pizza with salt and drizzle with oil.

6) Give the peel a quick shake to be sure the pizza is not sticking to the peel. Slide the pizza off the peel onto the stone in the oven. Broil for 1 minute. Turn the oven temperature to the highest bake setting and cook for 5 minutes. Quickly open the oven door, pull out the rack, and with a pair of tongs, rotate the pizza (not the stone) a half turn. Cook for 4 minutes more.

7) Using the peel, remove the pizza from the oven. Sprinkle with the remaining Parmesan cheese and drizzle with a little more olive oil. Cut into slices and serve.

MAKES ONE 12-INCH
(30 CM) PIZZA

6 extra-jumbo shrimp
(16 to 20 per pound)

2 shallots

1 ball New York or
Neapolitan–Style Pizza
Dough (page 31 or 35)

Cornmeal, for sprinkling

3 cups (60 g) loosely
packed baby arugula

1½ teaspoons grated
lemon zest

1 tablespoon (4 g)
chopped fresh dill

¼ cup plus 1 tablespoon
(30 g) freshly grated
Parmesan cheese

Kosher salt, to taste

Olive oil, for drizzling

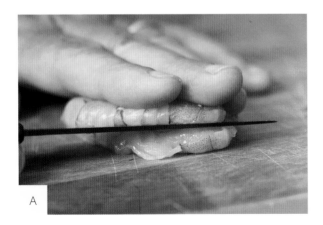

A

B

SMOKED SALMON

This pizza version of lox and bagels will compete for a place on your Sunday brunch table. It's best in the summer during fresh tomato season, but you can substitute cherry tomatoes at other times of the year or Fresh Tomato Sauce (page 43) using basil in place of the garlic and oregano.

1) Place a pizza stone on the top rack of a cool oven. Set the oven to broil and preheat for 30 minutes.

2) In a small bowl, stir together the mascarpone and cream cheeses. Mix in the lemon zest and half of the lemon juice. Season with salt and pepper.

3) On a generously floured work surface, flatten the dough ball with your fingertips and stretch it into a 12-inch (30 cm) round. (See page 13.)

4) Sprinkle a pizza peel with cornmeal and lay the pizza dough round on it. Spread the cheese mixture onto the pizza dough, leaving ½ to ¾ inch (1.3 to 2 cm) of dough uncovered around the outside edge. Cut the tomato slices in half and arrange them on top of the cheese. Sprinkle the scallions and capers on top of the tomatoes (**A**). Drizzle with oil.

5) Give the peel a quick shake to be sure the pizza is not sticking to the peel. Slide the pizza off the peel onto the stone in the oven. Broil for 1 minute. Turn the oven temperature to the highest bake setting and cook for 5 minutes. Quickly open the oven door, pull out the rack, and with a pair of tongs, rotate the pizza (not the stone) a half turn. Cook for 5 minutes more.

6) Meanwhile, cut the lettuce leaves crosswise into 1-inch-wide (2.5 cm) pieces. In a small bowl, toss the lettuce with the 1 teaspoon oil and the remaining lemon juice. Season with salt and pepper.

7) Using the peel, remove the pizza from the oven. Lay slices of the smoked salmon evenly over the pizza. Scatter the lettuce over the salmon. Cut into slices and serve.

A

MAKES ONE 12-INCH (30 CM) PIZZA

2 ounces (55 g) mascarpone cheese

2 ounces (55 g) cream cheese

1 teaspoon lemon zest

Juice of 1 lemon

Kosher salt, to taste

Freshly ground black pepper, to taste

1 ball New York–Style, Neapolitan–Style, or Paradiso Pizza Dough (page 31, 35, or 27)

Cornmeal, for sprinkling

5 slices from a medium tomato

¼ cup (25 g) sliced scallion

2 tablespoons (17 g) capers

1 teaspoon olive oil, plus more for drizzling

4 to 6 romaine lettuce leaves, preferably from the inner heart

2½ ounces (70 g) smoked salmon, sliced

TUNA

A fresh take on pizza, this makes a wonderfully light lunch or dinner. Feel free to substitute your favorite type of fish in place of the tuna. If you buy sushi-grade fish, you can replace the chunks of tuna with thinly cut slices of fish laid on top of the pizza after it emerges from the oven. The fish will cook only slightly from the heat of the pizza.

1) Place a pizza stone on the top rack of a cool oven. Set the oven to broil and preheat for 30 minutes.

2) Cut the tuna into 1-inch (2.5 cm) cubes and place in a bowl. Add lime zest, oil, salt, and a few grindings of pepper. Turn the tuna in the marinade. Let stand for 15 minutes.

3) On a floured work surface, flatten the dough ball with your fingertips and stretch it into a 12-inch (30 cm) round. (See page 13.)

4) Sprinkle a pizza peel with cornmeal and lay the dough round on it. Spread the Cilantro Pesto onto the dough, leaving ½ to ¾ inch (1.3 to 2 cm) of dough uncovered around the edge. Scatter the tomatoes on top of the pesto. Arrange the tuna and rings of onion evenly on top of the pesto and tomatoes. Sprinkle with salt and drizzle with oil.

5) Give the peel a quick shake to be sure the pizza is not sticking to it. Slide the pizza off the peel onto the stone in the oven. Broil for 1 minute. Turn oven temperature to the highest bake setting and cook for 5 minutes. Open the oven door, pull out the rack, and with a pair of tongs, rotate the pizza (not the stone) a half turn. Cook for 5 minutes more.

MAKES ONE
12-INCH (30 CM)
PIZZA

=====

6 to 7 ounces (170 to 200 g) fresh tuna

Zest of 1 lime

2 teaspoons olive oil, plus more for drizzling

Kosher salt, to taste

Freshly ground black pepper, to taste

1 ball Paradiso, New York–Style, or Neapolitan–Style Pizza Dough (page 27, 31, or 35)

Cornmeal, for sprinkling

⅔ cup (175 g) Cilantro Pesto

¾ cup (113 g) halved cherry tomatoes

5 very thin slices red onion

½ avocado

½ teaspoon freshly squeezed lime juice

6) Meanwhile, pit and peel the avocado. Cut into 12 to 15 thin slices and place in a small bowl. Add the lime juice, a drizzle of oil, a pinch of salt, and a few grindings of pepper. Turn the avocado slices in the dressing.

7) Using the peel, remove the pizza from the oven. Arrange the avocado slices evenly on top of the pizza. Cut into slices and serve.

Cilantro Pesto

1) Place the cilantro, jalapeño, garlic, lime zest, and lime juice in the bowl of a food processor. Process until finely chopped.

2) Add the salt, a few grindings of black pepper, and the cheese and process until blended. With the motor running, slowly add the olive oil.

3) Store in the refrigerator for up to 3 days.

MAKES ⅔ CUP
(175 G)

=====

3 ½ cups (56 g) loosely packed fresh cilantro

1 jalapeño pepper, seeds removed

2 cloves garlic

Zest of 2 limes and juice of 1 lime

¼ teaspoon kosher salt

Freshly ground black pepper to taste

¼ cup plus 2 tablespoons (35 g) freshly grated Parmesan cheese

2 tablespoons (28 ml) olive oil

Greg's Beer Cooler: Imperial Red Ale

Discordant looking, perhaps, but together the intensely pine-centric ale and herbaceous pesto reach unimagined heights.
Greg's Pick: Oskar Blues G'Knight

CHICKPEAS

Stepping outside of the world of the ordinary, this pizza enters a cross-cultural
dimension. You can use fresh, dried, or canned chickpeas for this pie. Just remember,
as with all beans, that they must be fully cooked before going on the pie.

1) Place a pizza stone on the top rack of a cool oven. Set the oven to broil and preheat for 30 minutes.

2) Cut 5 very thin slices of onion and set aside. Cut the rest into ¼-inch (6 mm) dice.

3) Heat the olive oil in a sauté pan over medium heat until warm. Add the diced onion and cook for 5 to 10 minutes or until soft. Turn the heat to low. Add the garlic and spices and cook for a minute or two until fragrant, stirring often. Add the chickpeas and 1 cup (225 g) of the Fresh Tomato Sauce. Season with salt and pepper and continue cooking for 10 to 15 minutes to develop the flavor. Remove from the heat when the sauce has reduced and coats the chickpeas, but before the mixture is dry (**A**). Let cool.

4) Finely grate one-quarter of the cucumber into a small bowl. You should have about ¼ cup (35 g) of cucumber. Add the yogurt, 2 teaspoons of the mint, 1 tablespoon (1 g) of the cilantro, and the milk and mix well. Season with salt and pepper and set aside.

5) Cut the remaining cucumber into ⅓-inch (about 1 cm) dice. Cut the feta cheese into ⅓-inch (about 1 cm) dice. You should have about ½ cup (85 g) of cheese.

6) On a floured work surface, flatten the dough ball with your fingertips and stretch it into a 12-inch (30 cm) round. (See page 13.)

7) Sprinkle a pizza peel with cornmeal and lay the pizza dough round on it. Spread the remaining ¾ cup (170 g) Fresh Tomato Sauce onto the pizza dough, leaving ½ to ¾ inch (1.3 to 2 cm) of dough uncovered around the outside edge. Spoon the chickpea mixture evenly over the sauce. Scatter ½ cup (70 g) diced cucumber on top of the chickpeas. Sprinkle with the remaining mint and cilantro. Scatter the cheese on top of the pizza. Arrange the rings of onion evenly on top of the cheese. Sprinkle the pizza with salt and drizzle with olive oil.

8) Give the peel a quick shake to be sure the pizza is not sticking to the peel. Slide the pizza off the peel onto the stone in the oven. Broil for 1 minute. Turn the oven temperature to the highest bake setting and cook for 5 minutes. Quickly open the oven door, pull out the rack, and with a pair of tongs rotate the pizza (not the stone) a half turn. Cook for 5 minutes more. Using the peel, remove the pizza from the oven.

9) Drizzle 2 tablespoons (28 g) of the yogurt mixture on top of the pizza. Cut into slices and serve with the remaining yogurt mixture on the side.

A

MAKES ONE 12-INCH (30 CM) PIZZA

1 medium onion, peeled

1 tablespoon (15 ml) olive oil, plus more for drizzling

½ teaspoon chopped garlic

1 teaspoon curry powder

Pinch each of ground coriander, cumin, and ginger

¾ cup (180 g) cooked chickpeas

1¾ cups (395 g) Fresh Tomato Sauce (page 43), divided

Kosher salt and freshly ground black pepper, to taste

1 large cucumber, peeled and seeded

½ cup (115 g) yogurt

1 tablespoon plus 2 teaspoons (10 g) chopped fresh mint

2 tablespoons (2 g) chopped fresh cilantro

2 tablespoons (28 ml) milk

3 ounces (85 g) feta cheese

1 ball Paradiso Pizza Dough (page 27)

Cornmeal, for sprinkling

TOFU

Pizza vacations in Asia in this recipe, with tofu, shiitake mushrooms, and bok choy as its companions and the tastes of the East—soy sauce, ginger, and sesame oil—as its souveniers. Substitute other proteins (chicken, pork, beef, or shrimp) for the tofu, if you prefer. Depending on the protein you choose to substitute, you may skip the roasting step.

1) Cut the tofu into ⅓-inch (about 1 cm) dice.

2) Whisk the soy sauce, the 2 teaspoons sesame oil, and 2 tablespoons (28 ml) of the olive oil. Stir in 1 teaspoon of the ginger, 1 teaspoon of the garlic, the red pepper flakes, a pinch of salt, and a grinding of pepper. Toss the tofu in the marinade and refrigerate for 24 hours.

3) Place a pizza stone on the top rack of a cool oven. Pre-heat your oven to 450°F (230°C, or gas mark 8).

4) Turn the tofu into a large roasting pan lined with alumi-num foil or a silicone baking liner and scatter it in a single layer. Roast for 15 to 25 minutes until nicely browned **(A)**. Remove the tofu from the oven and cool.

5) Set the oven to broil and preheat the pizza stone for 30 minutes.

6) Remove the stems from the mushrooms and discard. Cut the mushroom caps into ½-inch (1.3 cm) slices.

7) Cut the bok choy leaves into ½-inch (1.3 cm) slices.

8) In a large sauté pan, heat the remaining olive oil over medium heat. When the oil is hot, add the mushrooms and cook for 5 minutes or until soft. Add the bok choy and cook for 2 minutes more.

9) Turn the heat to low and add the remaining ½ teaspoon garlic and ½ teaspoon ginger. Season with salt and pepper and continue cooking for 2 to 3 minutes more, stirring often to ensure the garlic does not burn **(B)**. Remove from the heat and cool.

MAKES ONE 12-INCH (30 CM) PIZZA

7 ounces (200 g) firm tofu, drained

1 tablespoon (15 ml) soy sauce

2 teaspoons toasted sesame oil, plus more for drizzling

¼ cup (60 ml) olive oil

1 ½ teaspoons grated fresh ginger

1 ½ teaspoons chopped garlic

¼ teaspoon crushed red pepper flakes

Kosher salt, to taste

Freshly ground black pepper, to taste

4 ounces (115 g) shiitake mushrooms

2 small heads baby bok choy

1 small fresh tomato

3 scallions

1 ball Paradiso or Whole Wheat Pizza Dough (page 27 or 42)

Cornmeal, for sprinkling

A

B

10) Cut the tomato into ¼-inch (6 mm) dice. You should have ½ cup (90 g) of tomato.

11) Trim the scallions and cut into ¼-inch (6 mm) slices.

12) On a floured work surface, flatten the dough ball with your fingertips and stretch it into a 12-inch (30 cm) round. (See page 13.)

13) Sprinkle a pizza peel with cornmeal and lay the pizza dough round on it. Scatter 1½ cups (340 g) of the mushroom and bok choy mixture on top of the pizza dough, leaving ½ to ¾ inch (1.3 to 2 cm) of dough uncovered around the outside edge. Scatter the tofu and ½ cup (90 g) of the tomato on top of the vegetables. Sprinkle the pizza with the scallions and salt and drizzle with sesame oil.

14) Give the peel a quick shake to be sure the pizza is not sticking to the peel. Slide the pizza off the peel onto the stone in the oven. Broil for 1 minute. Turn the oven temperature to the highest bake setting and cook for 5 minutes. Quickly open the oven door, pull out the rack, and with a pair of tongs, rotate the pizza (not the stone) a half turn. Cook for 5 minutes more.

15) Using the peel, remove the pizza from the oven. Drizzle with sesame oil, cut into slices, and serve.

VEGETABLES

What better way to eat your vegetables than to include them as a topping on the world's favorite food? We've explored the familiar—onions, spinach, sweet peppers, artichokes, and mushrooms—but there are fields of vegetables yet to harvest.

We start this level simply, by dressing up a goat cheese and tomato pizza with an arugula salad. This light, summery pizza contrasts with the autumnual pumpkin pizza of Lesson 2, which appears on the Pizzeria Paradiso special menu every October.

We also work with cauliflower, broccoli rabe, fennel, and asparagus, employing various methods of cooking. Combined with a variety of complementary herbs, spices, cheeses, and accents, these recipes will inspire you to cultivate a farmer's bounty of new pizza choices.

ARUGULA

This is a pizza-and-salad combination—literally! Leafy vegetables like arugula can be used raw, as in this pizza, or cooked. You can dress the leaves as we do here or simply add them naked. You can also precook the vegetable with herbs, onions, or spices for a deeper, more complex taste.

1) Place a pizza stone on the top rack of a cool oven. Set the oven to broil and preheat for 30 minutes.

2) Break the goat cheese into ½-inch (1.3 cm) pieces. Set aside.

3) Place the vinegar, mustard, and garlic in a small bowl and whisk to combine. Whisk the oil into the vinegar mixture. Season with salt and pepper. Set the dressing aside.

4) On a floured work surface, flatten the dough ball with your fingertips and stretch it into a 12-inch (30 cm) round. (See page 13.)

5) Sprinkle a pizza peel with cornmeal and lay the pizza dough round on it. Spread the tomato sauce onto the pizza dough, leaving ½ to ¾ inch (1.3 to 2 cm) of dough uncovered around the outside edge. Sprinkle the pine nuts and parsley over the sauce. Scatter the cheese on top of the pizza **(A)**. Arrange the rings of onion evenly over the cheese. Sprinkle the pizza with salt and drizzle with oil.

6) Give the peel a quick shake to be sure the pizza is not sticking to the peel. Slide the pizza off the peel onto the stone in the oven. Broil for 1 minute. Turn the oven temperature to the highest bake setting and cook for 5 minutes. Quickly open the oven door, pull out the rack, and with a pair of tongs, rotate the pizza (not the stone) a half turn. Cook for 5 minutes more.

7) Using a pizza peel, remove the pizza from the oven. Cut into slices.

8) Whisk the dressing to combine. In a bowl, toss the arugula with a pinch of salt, a grinding of pepper, and the dressing.

9) Place the arugula on top of the pizza and serve.

MAKES ONE 12-INCH (30 CM) PIZZA

4 ounces (115 g) fresh goat cheese

½ teaspoon red wine vinegar

⅛ teaspoon Dijon mustard

One ¼ inch (6 mm)-thick slice garlic

1½ teaspoons olive oil, plus more for drizzling

Kosher salt to taste

Freshly ground black pepper to taste

1 ball Paradiso or Whole Wheat Pizza Dough (page 27 or 42)

Cornmeal, for sprinkling

¾ cup (170 g) Fresh Tomato Sauce (page 43) or Winter Tomato Sauce (page 28)

2 tablespoons (18 g) pine nuts

1 tablespoon (4 g) chopped fresh Italian parsley

5 very thin slices red onion

3 cups (60 g) loosely packed baby arugula

A

PUMPKIN

This recipe uses pureed pumpkin in combination with sage and ricotta cheese (a classic Italian trio), but the technique applies to all winter squashes, as well as to sweet potatoes. Alternatively, cut these vegetables into chunks and sauté, blanch, or roast them before topping your pizza. The key is that they must be fully cooked prior to adorning a pizza.

1) Place a pizza stone on the top rack of a cool oven. Set the oven to broil and preheat for 30 minutes.

2) Place the pumpkin puree, ricotta cheese, pine nuts, and sage in a small bowl. Season with the $1/4$ teaspoon salt and a few grindings of pepper. Mix well **(A)**.

3) Cut the bacon into $1/3$-inch (about 1 cm) pieces. In a small sauté pan, cook over medium heat until the bacon loses some of its fat and begins to brown. Drain the bacon on paper towels and set aside to cool.

4) On a floured work surface, flatten the dough ball with your fingertips and stretch it into a 12-inch (30 cm) round. (See page 13.)

5) Sprinkle a pizza peel with cornmeal and lay the pizza dough round on it. Spread the pumpkin mixture onto the pizza dough, leaving $1/2$ to $3/4$ inch (1.3 to 2 cm) of dough uncovered around the outside edge. Scatter the bacon on top of the pumpkin mixture. Sprinkle with the Parmesan cheese. Arrange the rings of onion evenly over the pizza. Sprinkle with salt and drizzle with oil.

6) Give the peel a quick shake to be sure the pizza is not sticking to the peel. Slide the pizza off the peel onto the stone in the oven. Broil for 1 minute. Turn the oven temperature to the highest bake setting and cook for 3 minutes. Quickly open the oven door, pull out the rack, and with a pair of tongs, rotate the pizza (not the stone) a half turn. Cook for 5 minutes more.

7) Using the peel, remove the pizza from the oven. Cut into slices and serve.

Note: When using diced vegetables in place of puree, double the amount of ricotta and do not add them to the ricotta mixture. Instead, add them to the pizza after the bacon.

Greg's Beer Cooler: Pumpkin Ale

Unlike many pumpkin beers on the market today, this pumpkin ale has flavors of fresh pumpkin, not pumpkin pie. These, earthy, savory, vegetal flavors perfectly complement the savory, salty notes of good slab bacon. More spice-focused pumpkin ales will pair as well, adding a spicy depth to the pizza.

Greg's Pick: Schlafly Pumpkin Ale

MAKES ONE 12-INCH
(30 CM) PIZZA

$2/3$ cup (163 g) cooked
pumpkin puree

$1/3$ cup (85 g) ricotta cheese

2 tablespoons (18 g) pine nuts

$1½$ teaspoons finely
chopped fresh sage

$1/4$ teaspoon kosher salt,
plus more for sprinkling

Freshly ground black
pepper, to taste

3 ounces (85 g) bacon

1 ball Paradiso Pizza
Dough (page 27)

Cornmeal, for sprinkling

$1/4$ cup (25 g) freshly grated
Parmesan cheese

5 very thin slices red onion

Olive oil, for drizzling

A

BROCCOLI RABE

This pie offers a fresh, simple combination of vegetables spiked with garlic and crushed red pepper flakes. Use this recipe as the base to develop seasonal pizzas to suit your tastes, substituting the freshest vegetables for the time of year in place of the broccoli rabe and cremini mushrooms. Complete the transformation by trying different cheeses as well.

1) Place a pizza stone on the top rack of a cool oven. Preheat the oven to 450°F (230°C, or gas mark 8).

2) Place the mushrooms and onions in a medium bowl. Add the 2 tablespoons (28 ml) olive oil, a pinch of salt, and a few grindings of pepper. Toss the onions and mushrooms until they are evenly coated with the oil, salt, and pepper.

3) Turn the mushrooms and onions into a large roasting pan lined with aluminum foil or a silicone baking liner. Scatter the vegetables in a single layer in the pan. Roast for 15 to 20 minutes or until the vegetables are soft and some pieces show significant browning. Remove the vegetables from the oven and cool. You should have about ¾ cup (170 g) of roasted vegetables.

4) Set the oven to broil and preheat the pizza stone for 30 minutes. Fill a medium pot two-thirds full with water and bring to a boil. Add salt until it tastes like salted water. Return to a boil.

5) Cut the end off each stem of broccoli rabe. Add the broccoli rabe to the boiling water and cook for 3 minutes. Remove from the heat, drain, and plunge the broccoli rabe into an ice water bath. When cool, drain again and lay on kitchen towels to dry.

6) Cut the broccoli rabe into 2-inch (5 cm) lengths. Cut the cheese into ⅓-inch (about 1 cm) dice. You should have about ¾ cup (115 g).

7) On a floured work surface, flatten the dough ball with your fingertips and stretch it into a 12-inch (30 cm) round. (See page 13.)

8) Sprinkle a pizza peel with cornmeal and lay the pizza dough round on it. Scatter the mushrooms and onions onto the pizza dough, leaving ½ to ¾ inch (1.3 to 2 cm) of dough uncovered around the outside edge. Arrange 1½ cups (60 g) of the broccoli rabe pieces evenly on top of the mushrooms and onions **(A)**. Sprinkle with the garlic and red pepper flakes. Scatter the cheese over the pizza. Sprinkle with salt and drizzle with olive oil.

9) Give the peel a quick shake to be sure the pizza is not sticking to the peel. Slide the pizza off the peel onto the stone in the oven. Broil for 1 minute. Turn the oven temperature to the highest bake setting and cook for 5 minutes. Quickly open the oven door, pull out the rack, and with a pair of tongs, rotate the pizza (not the stone) a half turn. Cook for 5 minutes more.

10) Using the peel, remove the pizza from the oven. Cut into slices and serve.

MAKES ONE 12-INCH (30 CM) PIZZA

4 ounces (115 g) cremini mushrooms, thickly sliced

1 small onion, thickly sliced

2 tablespoons (28 ml) olive oil, plus more for drizzling

Kosher salt, to taste

Freshly ground black pepper to taste

1 bunch broccoli rabe

4 ounces (115 g) Pecorino Toscano cheese (see page 21)

1 ball Paradiso Pizza Dough (page 27)

Cornmeal, for sprinkling

1 teaspoon chopped garlic

Pinch of crushed red pepper flakes

A

CAULIFLOWER

The unique flavor of cauliflower shines in this pizza. Spiked with onion, garlic, and thyme and highlighted by the smoky flavor of the mozzarella and speck (a smoked Italian ham), this pizza gives this sometimes overlooked ingredient its due. For a subtler pizza, blanch the cauliflower instead of roasting it.

1) Place a pizza stone on the top rack of a cool oven. Preheat your oven to 450°F (230°C, or gas mark 8).

2) Place the cauliflower in a medium bowl and toss with 1 teaspoon of the oil, a healthy pinch of salt, and a grinding of pepper.

3) Turn the cauliflower into a large roasting pan lined with aluminum foil or a silicone baking liner and spread it in a single layer. Roast for 15 to 25 minutes, until the cauliflower is soft and some pieces show significant browning. Remove the cauliflower from the oven and cool.

4) Set the oven to broil and preheat the pizza stone for 30 minutes. In a medium sauté pan, heat 1 tablespoon (15 ml) oil over medium heat until warm. Add the onions and cook for 5 to 10 minutes, or until soft.

5) Turn the heat to low and add the garlic and thyme. Cook for another minute or two until fragrant, stirring often to ensure the garlic does not burn. Remove from the heat.

6) In a large bowl, toss the cauliflower with the onion mixture (A). Season with salt and pepper.

7) Cut the cheese into ⅓-inch (about 1 cm) dice. You should have about ¾ cup (115 g).

8) On a floured work surface, flatten the dough ball with your fingertips and stretch it into a 12-inch (30 cm) round. (See page 13.)

9) Sprinkle a pizza peel with cornmeal and lay the pizza dough round on it. Scatter the cauliflower and onion mixture onto the pizza dough, leaving ½ to ¾ inch (1.3 to 2 cm) of dough uncovered around the outside edge. Sprinkle the parsley and scatter the cheese over the pizza. Sprinkle with salt and drizzle with olive oil.

10) Give the peel a quick shake to be sure the pizza is not sticking to the peel. Slide the pizza off the peel onto the stone in the oven. Broil for 1 minute. Turn the oven temperature to the highest bake setting and cook for 5 minutes. Quickly open the oven door, pull out the rack, and with a pair of tongs, rotate the pizza (not the stone) a half turn. Cook for 5 minutes more.

11) Using the peel, remove the pizza from the oven. Tear the speck slices into wide strips and lay them over the top of the pizza. Cut into slices and serve.

MAKES ONE 12-INCH
(30 CM) PIZZA

2 cups (200 g) small cauliflower florets

4 teaspoons (20 ml) olive oil, plus more for drizzling

Kosher salt, to taste

Freshly ground black pepper, to taste

1 cup (160 g) chopped onion

1 teaspoon chopped garlic

½ teaspoon chopped fresh thyme

4 ounces (115 g) smoked mozzarella

1 ball Paradiso Pizza Dough (page 27)

Cornmeal, for sprinkling

1 tablespoon (4 g) chopped fresh Italian parsley

4 slices speck

A

FENNEL

I love fennel for its subtle licorice flavor, and I love Italian oil-cured olives for their concentrated meaty flavor. Add orange to those two great flavors, as you will in this pizza, and you have a triple play. In addition to its bright, delightful taste, this pizza demonstrates a method for preparing vegetables, like fennel, that respond well to long and slow cooking.

1) Place a pizza stone on the top rack of a cool oven. Preheat your oven to 350°F (180°C, or gas mark 4).

2) Cut the stems and the bottom of the root end from the fennel bulb and discard. Trim away any brown edges from the outside layer. Cut the bulb in half from top to root. Cut each half into 4 wedges. In a bowl, toss the fennel wedges gently with the 1 teaspoon olive oil, a pinch of salt, and a few grindings of pepper. Lay the fennel in a single layer in a baking dish.

3) In a small pot, heat the orange juice and chicken stock together with a pinch of salt and a grinding of pepper. Bring the mixture to a boil. Remove from the heat and pour the mixture over the fennel. Cover the dish tightly with a piece of foil. Bake for 30 to 40 minutes until the fennel is soft when pierced with a fork. Remove the fennel from the oven and cool. With a slotted spoon, remove the fennel from the braising liquid and place on a plate. Set aside.

4) Set the oven to broil and preheat the pizza stone for 30 minutes.

5) Dice the feta cheese into ⅓-inch (about 1 cm) pieces. You should have about ½ cup (85 g).

6) On a floured work surface, flatten the dough ball with your fingertips and stretch it into a 12-inch (30 cm) round. (See page 13.)

7) Sprinkle a pizza peel with cornmeal and lay the pizza dough round on it. Arrange the fennel wedges on top of the pizza dough, leaving ½ to ¾ inch (1.3 to 2 cm) of dough uncovered around the outside edge. Sprinkle the fennel with the parsley and orange zest. Scatter the orange supremes, olives, and cheese on top of the fennel. Arrange the rings of onion evenly over the pizza. Sprinkle the pizza with salt and drizzle with oil.

8) Give the peel a quick shake to be sure the pizza is not sticking to the peel. Slide the pizza off the peel onto the stone in the oven. Broil for 1 minute. Turn the oven temperature to the highest bake setting and cook for 5 minutes. Quickly open the oven door, pull out the rack, and with a pair of tongs, rotate the pizza (not the stone) a half turn. Cook for 5 minutes more. Using the peel, remove the pizza from the oven. Cut into slices and serve.

MAKES ONE
12-INCH (30 CM)
PIZZA

2 small fennel bulbs

1 teaspoon olive oil, plus more for drizzling

Kosher salt, to taste

Freshly ground black pepper, to taste

½ cup (120 ml) freshly squeezed orange juice

½ cup (120 ml) chicken stock

3 ounces (85 g) feta cheese

1 ball Neapolitan–Style, Paradiso, or New York–Style Pizza Dough (page 35, 27, or 31)

Cornmeal, for sprinkling

1 tablespoon (4 g) chopped fresh Italian parsley

Zest of 1 orange

12 to 15 orange supremes (see page 23)

¼ cup (25 g) oil-cured Italian olives, pitted and halved (page 23)

5 very thin slices red onion

ROOTS AND GREENS

A full, woodsy flavor bursts from this pizza, making it perfect for a chilly fall evening's meal. I recommend a hearty crust to carry it. If you make this as a deep-dish pie, add 3 ounces (85 g) extra cheese, slice the cheese instead of dicing, and put some under and on top of the vegetables. If using the gluten-free crust, you will not need the full amount of each topping, since that crust makes a 9-inch (23 cm) pie.

1) Place a pizza stone on the top rack of a cool oven. Preheat your oven to 450°F (230°C, or gas mark 8).

2) Wash the beet and wrap it in aluminum foil. Put the wrapped beet in a small baking dish. Roast the beet in the oven for about 1 hour or until it is tender when pierced with a fork. When cool, peel and cut the beet into ⅓-inch (about 1 cm) dice.

3) Peel the turnip and cut into ⅓-inch (about 1 cm) dice. Cut the leek (white and pale green parts only) crosswise into ¼-inch (6 mm) slices and wash thoroughly under running water. Place the turnips and leeks in a medium bowl and toss with 1 teaspoon oil, a pinch of salt, and a grinding of pepper.

4) Turn the vegetables into a large roasting pan lined with aluminum foil or a silicone baking liner and scatter them in a single layer. Roast for 15 to 25 minutes until they are soft and some pieces show significant browning. Remove the vegetables from the oven and cool.

5) Set the oven to broil and preheat the pizza stone for 30 minutes.

6) Cut the cheese into ⅓-inch (about 1 cm) dice. You should have about ¾ cup (115 g).

7) In a large sauté pan, heat 2 teaspoons of oil over medium heat. When the oil is hot, add the greens. Turn the greens over in the pan continuously until the greens have wilted. Season with salt and pepper. Remove from the heat and cool.

8) On a floured work surface, flatten the dough ball with your fingertips and stretch it into a 12-inch (30 cm) round. (See page 13 for Whole Wheat or Multigrain dough, page 51 for Deep Dish, or page 38 for Gluten-Free.)

9) Sprinkle a pizza peel with cornmeal and lay the pizza dough round on it. Scatter the greens on top of the pizza dough, leaving ½ to ¾ inch (1.3 to 2 cm) of dough uncovered around the outside edge. Scatter ½ cup (113 g) beets and ¾ cup (170 g) turnips and leeks on top of the greens. Scatter the cheese on top of the vegetables. Sprinkle the pizza with salt and drizzle with oil.

10) Give the peel a quick shake to be sure the pizza is not sticking to the peel. Slide the pizza off the peel onto the stone in the oven. Broil for 1 minute. Turn the oven temperature to the highest bake setting and cook for 5 minutes. Quickly open the oven door, pull out the rack, and with a pair of tongs, rotate the pizza (not the stone) a half turn. Cook for 5 minutes more. Using the peel, remove the pizza from the oven. Cut into slices and serve.

MAKES ONE 12-INCH (30 CM) PIZZA

1 medium beet

1 small purple-top turnip

1 leek

1 tablespoon (15 g) olive oil, plus more for drizzling

Kosher salt, to taste

Freshly ground black pepper, to taste

4 ounces (115 g) Gruyère cheese

1½ cups (about 100 g) loosely packed greens (such as kale, Swiss chard, or a mix), stems removed

1 ball Whole Wheat, Multigrain, Deep-Dish, or Gluten-Free Pizza Dough (page 42, 46, 50, or 38)

Cornmeal, for sprinkling

Greg's Beer Cooler: Bière de Garde

This pairing of garden produce with a farmhouse ale unites the rustic flavors of hearty vegetables with those found in the flower garden—a perfect provincial marriage.

Greg's Pick: Stillwater Débutante

ASPARAGUS

The bright flavors of tarragon and lemon enhance the taste of the asparagus and sing of springtime. For a deeper flavor profile, roast larger pieces of asparagus and scatter them on the pizza instead of using the sliced raw asparagus.

1) Place a pizza stone on the top rack of a cool oven. Set the oven to broil and preheat the pizza stone for 30 minutes.

2) Grasp each asparagus spear and bend it until it breaks. Discard the bottom piece. Cut each spear into thin slices on the diagonal. Place the asparagus in a mixing bowl and toss it with the 1 teaspoon oil, salt, and pepper. You should have 1 1/4 cups (168 g) sliced asparagus.

3) Cut the tomato into 1/4-inch (6 mm) dice, discarding the core. You should have about 1/2 cup (90 g).

4) Cut the cheese into 1/3-inch (about 1 cm) dice. You should have about 3/4 cup (115 g).

5) On a floured work surface, flatten the dough ball with your fingertips and stretch it into a 12-inch (30 cm) round. (See page 13.)

6) Sprinkle a pizza peel with cornmeal and lay the pizza dough round on it. Scatter the asparagus pieces onto the pizza dough, leaving 1/2 to 3/4 inch (1.3 to 2 cm) of dough uncovered around the outside edge **(A)**. Scatter the diced tomato on top of the asparagus. Sprinkle with the tarragon. Scatter the cheese evenly over the pizza. Arrange rings of onion evenly on top of the cheese. Sprinkle the pizza with salt and drizzle with oil.

7) Give the peel a quick shake to be sure the pizza is not sticking to the peel. Slide the pizza off the peel onto the stone in the oven. Broil for 1 minute. Turn the oven temperature to the highest bake setting and cook for 5 minutes. Quickly open the oven door, pull out the rack, and with a pair of tongs, rotate the pizza (not the stone) a half turn. Cook for 5 minutes more.

8) Using the peel, remove the pizza from the oven. Sprinkle the lemon zest over the top of the pizza. Cut into slices and serve.

Note: Be sure to cut the asparagus very thinly. If the asparagus is cut too thick, then it will not cook thoroughly in the oven.

MAKES ONE 12-INCH (30 CM) PIZZA

10 spears asparagus

1 teaspoon olive oil, plus more for drizzling

Kosher salt, to taste

Freshly ground black pepper, to taste

1 small fresh tomato

4 ounces (115 g) Fontina cheese

1 ball Paradiso or Whole Wheat Pizza Dough (page 27 or 42)

Cornmeal, for sprinkling

1 teaspoon finely chopped fresh tarragon

5 very thin slices red onion

Zest of 1 lemon

A

FRUITS

When you saw the title of this level, did you think, *"Fruit?"* I understand, but recall that tomato is a fruit. So, will you find tomatoes in this level? Well, no, but you will find both savory and sweet fruit pizzas.

If we focus on the "pie" in "pizza pie," then fruit pizza makes perfect sense. So, cherries, berries, and banana cream pizza suddenly sound delicious.

The savory might require you to stretch your imagination. Can you imagine a pizza topped with apples, Brussels sprouts, and mushrooms? If you can't, I want to assure you that this pizza makes a regular appearance on Pizzeria Paradiso's specials list, and our customers, if you'll excuse me, eat it up. Still not convinced? Perhaps cantaloupe and prosciutto, pears and cheese, or lamb and apricots will stimulate your taste buds.

After you've made your way through these fruit pizzas, continue the trend and challenge yourself to use toppings in ways that will make you question your definition of them. Why not start by creating a dessert pizza using tomatoes and thereby turning the classic, ordinary topping into a new and exciting one?

CANTALOUPE

A perfect combination of salt and sweet, prosciutto and melon unite in a pie that's enhanced by the muskiness of buffalo mozzarella and brightened by mint and basil. You will delight in this pizza variation on the classic Italian antipasto. You can also make this pizza by adding the prosciutto along with the cantaloupe, after the pizza emerges from the oven.

1) Place a pizza stone on the top rack of a cool oven. Set the oven to broil and preheat for 30 minutes.

2) Cut the rind from the cantaloupe, remove the seeds, and cut the fruit into 9 or 10 thin slices. Set aside.

3) On a floured work surface, flatten the dough ball with your fingertips and stretch it into a 12-inch (30 cm) round. (See page 13.)

4) Sprinkle a pizza peel with cornmeal and lay the pizza dough round on it. Lay the prosciutto slices onto the pizza dough, leaving ½ to ¾ inch (1.3 to 2 cm) of dough uncovered around the outside edge. Sprinkle the prosciutto with 3 teaspoons (6 g) of the mint. Scatter the basil and mozzarella on top of the pizza (A). Arrange the rings of onion evenly over the other ingredients. Sprinkle with salt and drizzle with oil.

5) Give the peel a quick shake to be sure the pizza is not sticking to the peel. Slide the pizza off the peel onto the stone in the oven. Broil for 1 minute. Turn the oven temperature to the highest bake setting and cook for 5 minutes. Quickly open the oven door, pull out the rack, and with a pair of tongs, rotate the pizza (not the stone) a half turn. Cook for 5 minutes more.

6) Using the peel, remove the pizza from the oven. Arrange the cantaloupe slices over the pizza. Sprinkle with the Parmesan cheese and the remaining mint. Cut into slices and serve.

MAKES ONE 12-INCH (30 CM) PIZZA

¼ cantaloupe

1 ball Paradiso or Neapolitan–Style Pizza Dough (page 27 or 35)

Cornmeal, for sprinkling

3 very thin slices prosciutto di Parma

5 teaspoons (10 g) chopped fresh mint leaves

4 or 5 large basil leaves, torn in half

3 ounces (85 g) fresh buffalo mozzarella, torn into 10 to 12 pieces

5 very thin slices red onion

Kosher salt, to taste

Olive oil, for drizzling

1 tablespoon (5 g) freshly grated Parmesan cheese

A

APPLES

This pizza captures the flavors of fall in each bite. I call for a Braeburn apple, but you may substitute any slightly tart apple. In fact, this recipe lends itself to variation. Think of it as paint-by-numbers instructions. Numbers one through four represent vegetable, herb, cheese, and fruit. Then substitute within each number to create a masterpiece of your own.

1) Place a pizza stone on the top rack of a cool oven. Preheat your oven to 450°F (230°C, or gas mark 8).

2) Place the Brussel sprouts in a bowl and toss with ¼ teaspoon of the thyme, 1 teaspoon of the oil, a pinch of salt, and a grinding of pepper. Turn the Brussels sprouts into a large roasting pan lined with aluminum foil or a silicone baking liner and scatter them in a single layer. Roast for 20 to 25 minutes until they are soft and some pieces show significant browning. Let cool.

3) Remove the stems from the mushrooms and discard. Cut the mushroom caps into 1-inch (2.5 cm) pieces. Place them in a medium bowl and toss with the remaining thyme, 1 tablespoon (15 ml) olive oil, a pinch of salt, and a grinding of pepper.

4) Turn the mushrooms into another roasting pan lined with aluminum foil or a silicone baking liner and scatter them in a single layer. Roast for 15 to 20 minutes until they are soft and some pieces show significant browning. Remove the mushrooms from the oven and cool. Combine the roasted Brussels sprouts and mushrooms. You should have about 1¼ cups (280 g).

5) Set the oven to broil and preheat the pizza stone for 30 minutes.

6) Cut the cheese into ⅓-inch (about 1 cm) dice. You should have about ¾ cup (115 g). Cut the apple into ⅓-inch (about 1 cm) dice, discarding the core. You should have about ¾ cup (113 g).

7) On a floured work surface, flatten the dough ball with your fingertips and stretch it into a 12-inch (30 cm) round. (See page 13.)

8) Sprinkle a pizza peel with cornmeal and lay the pizza dough round on it. Scatter the Brussels sprouts and mushrooms on top of the pizza dough, leaving ½ to ¾ inch (1.3 to 2 cm) of dough uncovered around the outside edge. Scatter the apples, then the cheese, on top of the vegetables (A). Arrange the rings of onion evenly over the cheese. Sprinkle with salt and drizzle with oil.

9) Give the peel a quick shake to be sure the pizza is not sticking to the peel. Slide the pizza off the peel onto the stone in the oven. Broil for 1 minute. Turn the oven temperature to the highest bake setting and cook for 5 minutes. Quickly open the oven door, pull out the rack, and with a pair of tongs, rotate the pizza (not the stone) a half turn. Cook for 5 minutes more.

10) Using the peel, remove the pizza from the oven. Cut into slices and serve.

MAKES ONE 12-INCH (30 CM) PIZZA

8 Brussels sprouts, trimmed and cut in half vertically

½ teaspoon finely chopped fresh thyme

4 teaspoons (20 ml) olive oil, plus more for drizzling

Kosher salt to taste

Freshly ground black pepper to taste

8 ounces (225 g) portabella mushrooms

4 ounces (115 g) cheddar cheese

1 medium Braeburn apple

1 ball Paradiso or Whole Wheat Pizza Dough (page 27 or 42)

Cornmeal, for sprinkling

5 very thin slices red onion

Greg's Beer Cooler: Oktoberfest

Watch the leaves change color, enjoy the toasty, slightly sweet flavors of a Märzen, and bite into the flavors of fall. This pairing is the best of autumn in the glass and on the plate.

Greg's Pick: Ayinger Oktober Fest-Märzen

APRICOTS AND DATES

We travel to North Africa with this pizza, so you want lamb sausage spiced with cumin, cinnamon, paprika, ginger, and the like. If you can't find any at a local specialty store, try asking your butcher for ground lamb shoulder and spice it yourself. If you can find fresh dates or apricots, substitute them for the dried and skip the blanching step.

1) Place a pizza stone on the top rack of a cool oven. Preheat your oven to 450°F (230°C, or gas mark 8).

2) Peel the sweet potato and cut into 1/3-inch (about 1 cm) dice. Place the potatoes in a small bowl and toss with the 1 teaspoon oil, a pinch of salt, and a grinding of pepper.

3) Turn the sweet potatoes into a large roasting pan lined with aluminum foil or a silicone baking liner and scatter them in a single layer in the pan. Roast for 25 to 35 minutes until they are soft and some pieces show significant browning. Remove the sweet potatoes from the oven and cool.

4) Set the oven to broil and preheat the pizza stone for 30 minutes.

5) Cut the cheese into 1/3-inch (about 1 cm) dice. You should have about 1/2 cup (85 g).

6) Cut the apricots and dates into 1/4-inch (6 mm) slices. Bring a small pot of water to just below a boil. Drop the fruit into the hot water and remove from the heat. Let sit for 10 seconds and then drain. Lay the fruit on a paper towel to dry.

7) On a floured work surface, flatten the dough ball with your fingertips and stretch it into a 12-inch (30 cm) round. (See page 13.)

8) Sprinkle a pizza peel with cornmeal and lay the pizza dough round on it. Scatter 1 cup (136 g) of the sweet potatoes on top of the pizza dough, leaving 1/2 to 3/4 inch (1.3 to 2 cm) of dough uncovered around the outside edge. Sprinkle the potatoes with the almonds and garlic. Scatter the fruit and cheese on top of the pizza (**A**). Arrange the rings of onion evenly over the cheese. Dot the pizza with small pieces of the lamb sausage. Sprinkle the pizza with salt and drizzle with oil.

9) Give the peel a quick shake to be sure the pizza is not sticking to the peel. Slide the pizza off the peel onto the stone in the oven. Broil for 1 minute. Turn the oven temperature to the highest bake setting and cook for 5 minutes. Quickly open the oven door, pull out the rack, and with a pair of tongs, rotate the pizza (not the stone) a half turn. Cook for 5 minutes more.

10) Using the peel, remove the pizza from the oven. Grate the zest of the lime over the pizza and sprinkle with the cilantro. Cut into slices and serve.

MAKES ONE 12-INCH (30 CM) PIZZA

1 small sweet potato

1 teaspoon olive oil, plus more for drizzling

Kosher salt, to taste

Freshly ground black pepper, to taste

3 ounces (85 g) feta cheese

3 whole dried apricots

4 whole dried dates

1 ball Paradiso or Whole Wheat Pizza Dough (page 27 or 42)

Cornmeal, for sprinkling

1/4 cup (25 g) chopped almonds

1 teaspoon chopped garlic

5 very thin slices red onion

2 1/2 ounces (70 g) bulk lamb sausage

1 lime

2 tablespoons (2 g) chopped fresh cilantro

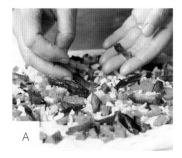

A

PEARS

Here fruit and cheese are paired with ginger and endive, calling to mind a wonderfully delicate composed hors d'oeuvre or cheese course. Bosc pears are my first choice for this pie, since even when ripe and cooked they retain their firm character. To ripen pears, place them in a brown paper bag for a couple of days.

1) Place a pizza stone on the top rack of a cool oven. Set the oven to broil and preheat the pizza stone for 30 minutes.

2) Trim any brown from the heads of endive. Cut the heads crosswise into ½-inch (1.2 cm) slices.

3) In a large sauté pan, heat the 2 tablespoons (15 ml) of oil over medium heat. When the oil is hot, add the onions and cook for 5 to 10 minutes or until soft. Add the endive and ginger and cook for 2 to 3 minutes more, stirring often to ensure the ginger does not burn. Season with salt and pepper. Remove from the heat and cool.

4) Cut the cheese into ⅓-inch-thick (about 1 cm) slices.

5) Trim the chives and cut into 1-inch (2.5 cm) lengths. You should have about 2 tablespoons (6 g).

6) On a floured work surface, flatten the dough ball with your fingertips and stretch it into a 12-inch (30 cm) round. (See page 13.)

7) Sprinkle a pizza peel with cornmeal and lay the pizza dough round on it. Scatter the endive on top of the pizza dough, leaving ½ to ¾ inch (1.3 to 2 cm) of dough uncovered around the outside edge. Sprinkle 1 tablespoon (3 g) of the chives over the endive. Arrange the pear slices and the cheese on top of the pizza **(A)**. Sprinkle with salt and drizzle with oil.

8) Give the peel a quick shake to be sure the pizza is not sticking to the peel. Slide the pizza off the peel onto the stone in the oven. Broil for 1 minute. Turn the oven temperature to the highest bake setting and cook for 5 minutes. Quickly open the oven door, pull out the rack, and with a pair of tongs, rotate the pizza (not the stone) a half turn. Cook for 5 minutes more.

9) Using the peel, remove the pizza from the oven. Sprinkle with the remaining chives, cut into slices, and serve.

Note: Sqeeze a little lemon juice on the pear slices to prevent them from browning as you build the pizza.

MAKES ONE 12-INCH
(30 CM) PIZZA

2 heads Belgian endive

2 tablespoons (15 ml) olive oil, plus more for drizzling

1 cup (160 g) chopped onion

1 tablespoon (8 g) grated fresh ginger

Kosher salt, to taste

Freshly ground black pepper, to taste

4 ounces (115 g) Taleggio cheese

7 to 9 fresh chives

1 ball Paradiso or Whole Wheat Pizza Dough (page 27 or 42)

Cornmeal, for sprinkling

1 small Bosc or Anjou pear, cored and cut into 12 to 15 thin slices

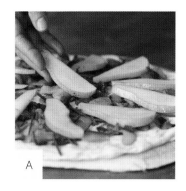

A

CHERRIES

Reminiscent of cannoli, this is a rich pie. The layers of flavor, from
rosemary and orange to chocolate and kirsch, make it complex and
not too sweet. Use frozen cherries when you can't get fresh.

1) Place a pizza stone on the top rack of a cool oven. Set the oven to broil and preheat for 30 minutes.

2) Cover the dried cherries with boiling water for 1 minute and then drain.

3) Grate ½ ounce (15 g) of the chocolate and set aside. Chop the remaining chocolate into small pieces.

4) Place the ricotta cheese in a medium bowl. Add the dried cherries, chopped chocolate, ginger, hazelnuts, walnuts, kirsch, orange zest, chopped rosemary, and salt. Stir to combine **(A)**.

5) Cut the fresh cherries in half.

6) On a floured work surface, flatten the dough ball with your fingertips and stretch it into a 12-inch (30 cm) round. (See page 13.)

7) Sprinkle a pizza peel with cornmeal and lay the pizza dough round on it. Spread the ricotta mixture onto the pizza dough, leaving ½ to ¾ inch (1.3 to 2 cm) of dough uncovered around the outside edge. Scatter the fresh cherries over the ricotta.

8) Give the peel a quick shake to be sure the pizza is not sticking to the peel. Slide the pizza off the peel onto the stone in the oven. Broil for 1 minute. Turn the oven temperature to the highest bake setting and cook for 5 minutes. Quickly open the oven door, pull out the rack, and with a pair of tongs, rotate the pizza (not the stone) a half turn. Cook for 5 minutes more.

9) Using the peel, remove the pizza from the oven. Cut into slices and dust with the confectioners' sugar. Sprinkle with the grated chocolate and serve.

MAKES ONE 12-INCH (30 CM) PIZZA

⅔ cup (107 g) dried cherries, chopped

3 ounces (85 g) bittersweet chocolate

1 cup (250 g) ricotta cheese

2 tablespoons (28 g) chopped candied ginger

2 tablespoons (14 g) coarsely chopped hazelnuts

2 tablespoons (15 g) coarsely chopped walnuts

3 tablespoons (45 ml) kirsch or brandy (optional)

1 tablespoon (6 g) grated orange zest

1 teaspoon very finely chopped fresh rosemary

Pinch of kosher salt

1 cup (155 g) fresh cherries, pitted

1 ball Paradiso, Neapolitan–Style, or New York–Style Pizza Dough (page 27, 35, or 31)

Cornmeal, for sprinkling

Confectioners' sugar, for dusting

A

BERRIES

This pizza starts with an almond-basil pesto. With its greenish brown hue, it may not seem like a good base for dessert, but trust me—basil and berries are a match made in heaven. Lemon and honey elevate this union into a sophisticated and delicious conclusion for any meal. Use smaller berries whole and slice or dice large berries into smaller pieces. A drizzle of honey finishes this pizza. Its flavor will be in the forefront, so choose a good quality honey with a flavor you enjoy.

1) Place a pizza stone on the top rack of a cool oven. Set the oven to broil and preheat for 30 minutes.

2) Place the whole almonds in the bowl of a food processor and process until coarsely chopped. Add the basil and lemon zest and process until finely chopped.

3) Add the cheese, the 2 tablespoons (40 g) of honey, and the salt and process until blended.

4) In a small bowl, toss half of the berries with a drizzle of honey. Set aside.

5) On a floured work surface, flatten the dough ball with your fingertips and stretch it into a 12-inch (30 cm) round. (See page 13.)

6) Sprinkle a pizza peel with cornmeal and lay the pizza dough round on it. Spread the almond-basil mixture onto the pizza dough, leaving ½ to ¾ inch (1.3 to 2 cm) of dough uncovered around the outside edge. Arrange the lemon supremes on top of the almond-basil mixture. Scatter the slivered almonds and the remaining berries over the pizza. Drizzle liberally with honey (**A**).

7) Give the peel a quick shake to be sure the pizza is not sticking to the peel. Slide the pizza off the peel onto the stone in the oven. Broil for 1 minute. Turn the oven temperature to the highest bake setting and cook for 3 minutes. Quickly open the oven door, pull out the rack, and with a pair of tongs, rotate the pizza (not the stone) a half turn. Cook for 3 minutes more.

8) Using the peel, remove the pizza from the oven. Drizzle liberally with honey and cut into slices.

9) Mound the reserved berries in the center of the pizza and serve.

Greg's Beer Cooler: Witbier

Pairing the quintessential summer beer, wheat beer, with this summertime pie makes for seasonal harmony. The subtle flavors of lemon, vanilla, and honey found in the Allagash complement the natural sugars and fresh fruit notes of the pizza. Other wheat beers will do the same, perhaps with a slightly different focus.

Greg's Pick: Allagash White

MAKES ONE 12-INCH (30 CM) PIZZA

½ cup (73 g) whole almonds

10 medium fresh basil leaves

Zest of 1 lemon

½ cup (120 g) mascarpone cheese

2 tablespoons (40 g) honey, plus more for drizzling

Pinch of kosher salt

2 cups (290 g) mixed fresh berries

1 ball Neapolitan–Style or New York–Style Pizza Dough (page 35 or 31)

Cornmeal, for sprinkling

12 to 15 lemon supremes (page 23)

¼ cup (28 g) slivered almonds

A

BANANAS

My mother makes really good pies. I think of this as an homage to her, combining two of my favorites (coconut custard and banana cream) in one. Overripe bananas will be easier to mash and will intensify the flavor. One bite and you'll thank my mom!

1) Place a pizza stone on the top rack of a cool oven. Set the oven to broil and preheat for 30 minutes.

2) In a medium bowl, mash 1 banana with a fork or potato masher until you have a smooth pulp. Stir the eggs, 1/4 cup (60 ml) of the heavy cream, 1/4 cup (21 g) of the coconut, the sugar, lime zest, a dash of vanilla, the rum, and salt into the mashed banana until well combined.

3) Place the remaining coconut in a small sauté pan. Over medium heat, toast the coconut until just golden. Shake the pan often to ensure the coconut does not burn.

4) Separately whip the remaining heavy cream until it forms soft peaks. Stir in a dash of vanilla and chill.

5) Cut the second banana into 1/3-inch (about 1 cm) pieces.

6) On a floured work surface, flatten the dough ball with your fingertips and stretch it into a 12-inch (30 cm) round. (See page 13.)

7) Sprinkle a pizza peel with cornmeal and lay the pizza dough round on it. Scatter the banana pieces onto the pizza dough, leaving 1/2 to 3/4 inch (1.3 to 2 cm) of dough uncovered around the outside edge.

8) Give the peel a quick shake to be sure the pizza is not sticking to the peel. Slide the pizza off the peel onto the stone in the oven. Broil for 1 minute. Quickly open the oven door and pull out the rack. Holding the rack level if necessary, carefully pour the banana-egg mixture onto the pizza by starting at the inside edge of the thickest part of the crust (**A**). If necessary, use a spatula or spoon to spread the mixture. Slide the rack back into the oven and close the oven door. Turn the oven temperature to the highest bake setting and cook for 5 minutes.

9) Again, quickly open the oven door, pull out the rack, and with a pair of tongs, rotate the pizza (not the stone) a half turn. Cook for 2 to 3 minutes more.

10) Using the peel, remove the pizza from the oven and cool for 15 minutes. Cut into slices and transfer to a serving platter.

11) Spoon the whipped cream onto the pizza. Sprinkle with the toasted coconut and serve.

MAKES ONE 12-INCH
(30 CM) PIZZA

2 bananas

2 large eggs

3/4 cup (175 ml) heavy cream

1/4 cup plus 2 tablespoons (32 g) shredded unsweetened coconut

1 tablespoon (13 g) sugar

1 teaspoon grated lime zest

2 dashes of vanilla extract

1 tablespoon (15 ml) rum

Pinch of kosher salt

1 ball Paradiso or New York–Style Pizza Dough (page 27 or 31)

Cornmeal, for sprinkling

A

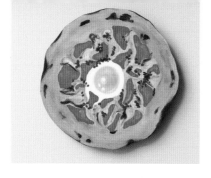  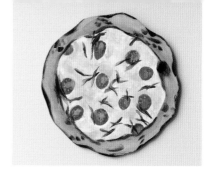

ACKNOWLEDGMENTS

First, a nod to my parents, who taught me to value love, thought, education, family, others, work, perseverance, and myself. Your consistent support of me, and my choices, has instilled in me a sense of security that is invaluable.

At my mother's side, I found a love of cooking and an understanding of the joy that food and nourishing others holds. From my father, I gained an innate sense of business, responsibility, leadership, and the power of negotiation. From my large family of big personalities, I have known comfort, strength, pain, and love. I thank you for standing with me and holding me, and each other, through all.

I want to acknowledge my Pizzeria Paradiso family as well. To say I am grateful does not adequately express the appreciation I feel for each and every one of our customers. I thank you for your continued loyalty and for the opportunity you repeatedly give to me, and the whole Pizzeria Paradiso staff, to nourish you again and again.

To my staff: You call me Momma, and while I graciously acknowledge that I represent that role to many of you, the relationship is reciprocal. I thank you for making Paradiso more than a job or a restaurant. Together we have created a community that thrives on respect, generosity, hard work, and fun. Thank you for every moment.

A special acknowledgment goes to my colleague Bonnie Moore for convincing me to write this book and then for helping me along the path. You did so many things, from providing a focused place for working, to pizza testing, to recipe editing, to concept tweaking, to friendship. I can't say how glad I am that you and your boys like pizza.

Finally, many individuals have helped, taught, and coaxed me along the way to today. I want to thank Madeleine Kamman for her knowledge and guidance; Midge and Dick Johnson for welcoming me into their family; Dean Madrid, Carlos Gonzales, Greg Jasgur, Sara Gunter, Veda Mitchell, Matt McQuilkin, Carl Sumter, and Scott Griswold for many years of help managing the Paradiso world; the women of WCR for embracing me; Carla Hall for her hard boiled egg peeling tip; Donna Packer-Kinlaw, for her editing skills; Laura Einstein for saving me and Paradiso many years ago; Tsigerda Fikak for her care; my pizza testers for their insights; Leanne Poteet for the compass; and Gail Persily and Elizabeth Wiley, with whom I have cooked, eaten, and realized so much of life. Last, and most, thank you, Barbara, for your love.

ABOUT THE AUTHOR

Owner and chef Ruth Gresser learned her craft at her mother's side, cooking for her large family and her mother's catering company. Ms. Gresser cooked her way through college before entering the professional food scene in San Francisco at the early stages of the modern American food movement. In 1987, after graduating summa cum laude from Madeleine Kamman's Classical and Modern French Cooking School, and cooking professionally in French, American, and Italian restaurants across the country, she moved to Washington, D.C.

In 1991, she turned her attention to pizza and opened Pizzeria Paradiso to critical acclaim. Now considered the matriarch of pizza in the District, Ms. Gresser has been instrumental to the opening of five popular Washington restaurants.

Gresser sits on the board of directors of Women Chefs and Restaurateurs, is a member of Les Dames d'Escoffier, and has been profiled in *The Washington Post Magazine* and *The Washington Business Journal*. She lives in Silver Spring, Maryland, where she recently married her partner of 21 years.

INDEX